Save Money using AI

The smartest way to cut costs isn't more spreadsheets, it's artificial intelligence.
Discover how AI can slash your bills, cancel traps, and keep more money in your pocket.

Written by

ERIC LEBOUTHILLIER

AcraSolution | 2025 1st Edition
www.acrasolution.com

Preface

Who this book is for

This book is written for anyone who feels trapped by rising costs, hidden fees, and the never-ending stream of subscription charges draining their bank account. It's for everyday people — students, professionals, parents, and even retirees — who want to finally take control of their money without becoming financial experts. Whether you're tired of wasting hours negotiating with service providers, frustrated by surprise bill hikes, or simply curious about how artificial intelligence can work for you, this book will show you a smarter, faster, and easier way to save.

What to expect from this book

Inside these pages, you'll discover a practical, step-by-step guide to putting your finances on autopilot. You'll learn how to use AI tools to scan for unnecessary charges, cancel free-trial traps before they cost you, cut down inflated bills, renegotiate better deals, and even recover money you didn't know you lost. Each chapter comes with simple checklists, ready-to-use scripts, and real-world examples that you can apply immediately — no jargon, no complex spreadsheets, and no guesswork. By the time you finish, you'll know exactly how to set up your own personal "money autopilot," saving you $1,000 or more each year while giving you back your time and peace of mind.

LEGAL DISCLAIMER

This publication is intended solely for informational and educational purposes. It does not constitute legal, financial, medical, or professional advice. The content is not a substitute for consultation with qualified experts or licensed professionals in the relevant fields.

Portions of this work have been created or assisted by artificial intelligence (AI) tools. While every reasonable effort has been made to review, fact-check, and edit the content for clarity and accuracy, AI-generated information may occasionally contain errors, omissions, or generalized statements. The author and publisher do not guarantee the accuracy, completeness, or reliability of the information provided.

Readers are strongly encouraged to seek independent advice tailored to their personal circumstances from qualified legal, financial, healthcare, or compliance professionals before making decisions or taking action based on this content.

References to specific products, services, companies, websites, or technologies do not imply endorsement or affiliation unless explicitly stated. All trademarks and brand names mentioned remain the property of their respective owners.

The author and publisher disclaim any liability, loss, or risk incurred directly or indirectly from the use or misuse of this publication. This includes, but is not limited to, damages of any kind — including incidental, special, or consequential — arising out of the reliance on the material presented.

All references to laws, regulations, security standards, or industry guidelines are intended for general awareness only and may not reflect the most current legal developments. This publication is not intended to create, and receipt does not constitute, a client relationship with the author, publisher, or any affiliated entity.

By reading, accessing, or applying the content in this publication, you agree to do so at your own risk. If you do not accept these terms, you are advised to discontinue use of this material immediately.

ROI Disclaimer

This book is intended for educational and informational purposes only. While the strategies, scripts, and tools described herein can help identify savings opportunities and reduce unnecessary expenses, results will vary depending on individual circumstances, financial habits, service providers, and market conditions. No guarantee of specific savings, income, or return on investment is made or implied. Readers are encouraged to use their own judgment and, where appropriate, consult qualified financial, legal, or tax professionals before taking action. The author and publisher disclaim any liability for financial decisions made based on the information provided in this book.

Table of Contents

INTRODUCTION

Why You're Losing $1,000+ a Year Without
Knowing It

The Hidden Leaks in Modern Life

Most people believe that if they aren't making large, impulsive purchases, their money is safe. They imagine that financial danger comes only from big-ticket items: a luxury car, a five-star vacation, or a sudden emergency expense. In reality, what drains most wallets are not the big splurges, but the quiet, invisible leaks that happen month after month.

Streaming subscriptions you forgot to cancel. Bank fees so small you barely notice them. Internet bills that creep up by a few dollars every year. These charges rarely trigger alarm bells, yet together, they silently drain **$1,000 or more annually from the average household**. The biggest problem? Most people don't even realize it's happening.

Death by a Thousand Small Charges

The psychology behind these leaks is simple: small amounts don't feel painful. Behavioral economists call this *"mental accounting"*— our brains treat a $6 charge as insignificant, even though twelve of those charges equal a full $72 a year. Add in another $15 subscription, a $35 "service fee," and a $120 insurance overcharge, and suddenly you're losing hundreds without ever making a conscious decision.

Companies know this. In fact, they design their billing systems around it. Free trials that automatically convert, "introductory" rates that expire without warning, fees hidden in fine print—these are not accidents. They are business models built on the assumption that you won't notice. And most people don't.

The Illusion of Control

Traditional budgeting methods fail here. A spreadsheet might help you track groceries or rent, but it won't flag that your internet bill quietly went up by $9 last month. You can't manually watch every line of every statement without dedicating hours every week. That's why so many people believe they are in control—while their money slips away in the background.

This is why the average American now pays for **over 7 active subscriptions** yet uses fewer than half of them. This is why banks earn billions annually from overdraft fees. This is why utilities and telecom companies consistently raise rates, knowing most customers won't bother calling to negotiate.

Where AI Changes the Equation

The leaks aren't going away—but technology gives you a way to fight back. Artificial Intelligence flips the equation by turning passive losses into active detection. Instead of you scanning every bill, AI can scan it for you. Instead of guessing which subscription is unused, AI can track your logins and spending patterns to highlight waste. Instead of blindly accepting a rate hike, AI can draft negotiation scripts—or even auto-chat with providers on your behalf.

In short: **AI replaces effort with action**. Where spreadsheets show you the past, AI acts on the present. It doesn't just highlight the leak; it plugs it.

The Cost of Ignoring the Leaks

Imagine leaving a faucet dripping in your kitchen. One drop doesn't matter. But over a year, you waste gallons of water and rack up higher bills. Money leaks work the same way: invisible, constant, and compounding.

Here's the reality: if you don't actively address them, you will continue to lose **$1,000–$2,000 every single year**. That's money that could go into an emergency fund, pay off debt faster, or cover a vacation without guilt. Every month you delay, you're letting companies profit from your inattention.

Takeaway: Hidden leaks are not a personal failing—they're a feature of modern financial systems designed to exploit human psychology. The good news? With AI, you finally have a tool that works as tirelessly as the companies trying to take your money. Instead of fighting blind, you can let automation catch what you can't see—and start reclaiming the hundreds you've been losing without even knowing it.

Why Traditional Budgeting Fails Most People

For decades, financial advice has been built around a single solution: make a budget and stick to it. On paper, it looks like a cure-all. Write down what you earn, list your expenses, and stay within the numbers. Simple, right? Yet studies show that **more than 70% of people who create a budget abandon it within a few months**. The reason isn't laziness or lack of willpower—it's that traditional budgeting is built for a world that no longer exists.

The Myth of Perfect Self-Discipline

Budgets assume people will act like machines: consistently recording, categorizing, and adjusting every purchase. But life is unpredictable. A flat tire, a birthday dinner, a forgotten subscription—all of these fall outside neat budget categories. Each "mistake" creates guilt, and guilt is the fastest way to make people quit.

Psychologists call this the *"abstinence violation effect"*: once someone slips up, they feel the system is broken and abandon it entirely. That's why so many people start the year with a color-coded spreadsheet and end the year avoiding their banking app altogether.

The Speed of Money vs. The Speed of Humans

Money moves faster than people can track it. Charges hit at odd times, subscriptions renew automatically, and prices rise without notice. A static spreadsheet or app is always playing catch-up. By the time you notice the change, the damage is done.

Take internet bills, for example. Providers often raise rates by $5–$10 every year. Unless you're carefully logging each bill and comparing it against last year's, you probably won't notice. Multiply that by utilities, insurance, and bank fees, and you see the problem: manual budgeting is a **rear-view mirror**. It tells you where you've been, not what's draining you right now.

Hidden Complexity No One Tracks

Another issue is that most budgets oversimplify spending. "Groceries" is one line, but in reality it's full of hidden patterns: overpaying for delivery fees, missing coupons, falling for dynamic pricing online. Traditional budgets can't uncover these invisible costs because they only track totals, not patterns.

It's like checking your car's fuel gauge without knowing there's a hole in the tank. You know the fuel is low, but not where or why it's disappearing.

Why AI Is Different

The failure of traditional budgeting isn't just about discipline—it's about tools. Humans aren't built to track dozens of micro-transactions across accounts. But AI is. It doesn't tire, it doesn't forget, and it doesn't overlook the $7.99 subscription you signed up for last winter.

Instead of asking you to manage everything yourself, AI monitors spending automatically. It flags anomalies, predicts future bills, and even acts on your behalf to cancel or renegotiate. Where traditional budgeting relies on memory and willpower, AI relies on data and automation. That shift changes everything.

Takeaway: Traditional budgeting fails because it assumes humans can track money with perfect discipline in an unpredictable, automated financial system. AI doesn't demand more willpower—it simply does the work for you. That's why people who hate budgeting still save money once they let technology step in.

How AI Flips the Equation: Action > Spreadsheets

For decades, money management advice has centered on spreadsheets, expense trackers, and budgeting apps. These tools are designed to *show you* where your money went. The problem? Awareness doesn't equal action. Knowing you overspent on takeout last month doesn't lower next month's delivery bill. Spreadsheets are mirrors—they reflect the past but can't change the present.

AI changes the game because it doesn't just *observe*—it *acts*.

From Passive Tracking to Active Guardrails

Traditional tools wait for you to do the work. You log in, enter data, categorize transactions, and promise yourself to "do better." AI eliminates that manual labor. It connects directly to your bank, credit card, and bill accounts, then continuously monitors for patterns.

If your internet bill quietly jumps by $12, AI flags it instantly. If you're still paying for a streaming service you haven't used in six months, AI suggests canceling—or cancels it for you with one click. Instead of passively tracking leaks, AI actively plugs them.

Think of it like cruise control in a car. A spreadsheet tells you that you sped last week. AI prevents you from speeding right now.

Automation Beats Willpower

Most financial systems fail because they rely on human discipline. But discipline is finite. By the end of a long day, the last thing you want to do is comb through receipts. AI removes that burden by automating decisions you'd otherwise avoid.

For example, some AI tools can auto-dispute bank fees, renegotiate bills with service providers, or apply digital coupons at checkout without you lifting a finger. Each small action might save only $5–$20, but combined, they add up to hundreds over the year—without requiring you to change behavior or develop "perfect" habits.

This is what psychologists call a *nudge system*: subtle changes in the environment that guide better outcomes without requiring extra effort. AI becomes your personal money nudge, always on, always watching.

Real-Time, Not Rear-View

The most powerful shift AI offers is real-time action. Instead of realizing in March that January was expensive, you get alerts and solutions as money moves.

If your spending is trending higher than usual this week, AI can suggest pausing nonessential purchases or moving funds to cover a shortfall. If a subscription trial is ending tomorrow, it can remind you—or auto-cancel before you're charged.

This transforms budgeting from a reactive chore into a proactive system. You don't just see what happened—you prevent what shouldn't happen.

Takeaway: Spreadsheets give you information. AI gives you results. By turning passive tracking into active intervention, AI removes the need for constant vigilance and replaces it with automation. The equation shifts: it's no longer about how disciplined you are—it's about how effectively your AI can act on your behalf.

Quick Preview of What This Book Will Help You Save

By the time you finish this book, you'll see your money differently—not as something you constantly chase, but as something quietly protected by systems that run on autopilot. The goal isn't just to *track* your finances, but to put real money back in your pocket with minimal effort.

Here's what you can expect to unlock:

Subscriptions You Don't Use

Most people pay for at least three recurring services they've forgotten about—streaming platforms, apps, memberships. AI tools can scan your bank statements and inbox to identify these "silent drainers," then help you cancel in minutes. Typical savings: **$200–$400 a year.**

Bills That Creep Up

Internet, phone, and utilities almost always rise quietly over time. AI can spot hikes the moment they happen and even draft negotiation scripts or chat with providers for you. Typical savings: **$300–$600 a year.**

Hidden Fees and Bank Charges

Overdraft fees, ATM charges, late-payment penalties—banks and credit cards profit heavily from your inattention. AI doesn't just flag them; in some cases it automatically disputes them. Typical savings: **$100–$300 a year.**

Insurance Overpayments

Loyalty in the insurance world often costs you. Rates drift upward while new customers get discounts. AI compares policies across providers, alerts you to better options, and helps you switch with minimal friction. Typical savings: **$200–$500 a year.**

Smarter Everyday Spending

From grocery markups to dynamic online pricing, AI can find hidden overcharges, apply coupons automatically, and optimize cashback and rewards programs. Typical savings: **$200–$400 a year.**

Scam and Fraud Protection

AI can monitor for suspicious subscriptions, fake vendors, and unusual charges 24/7—shielding you from financial losses that could cost far more than the "small leaks." Typical savings: **Peace of mind, plus hundreds saved from avoided fraud.**

Add it up: even on the conservative end, most readers will reclaim **$1,000+ every year**—without adding hours of work or adopting a new lifestyle. That's money you can use to build savings, pay down debt, or fund experiences that actually matter.

Takeaway: This book isn't about cutting out your morning coffee or denying yourself small joys. It's about eliminating the waste that companies hope you never notice. With AI on your side, you stop playing defense with your money and start letting automation fight for you—every single day.

CHAPTER 1

Finding the Leaks: Understanding Where Money Disappears

The Psychology of "Small Charges" That Add Up

When people imagine financial problems, they often picture one catastrophic event: a lost job, a medical emergency, or a big purchase they couldn't afford. But for most households, money doesn't disappear in one dramatic moment—it leaks away through dozens of small, almost invisible charges. A $7 streaming service here. A $15 app there. A $4 "processing fee" you didn't notice. None of these sting on their own, but together they create a steady drain that empties your wallet year after year.

Why Small Amounts Feel Harmless

Psychologists call this *denomination neglect*: our brains struggle to treat small sums with the same seriousness as large ones. Spending $50 feels like a decision. Spending $5 feels like nothing. Yet ten of those $5 charges equal the same $50—but without the mental "alarm" that usually makes us pause.

This effect is amplified when payments are automatic. You don't hand over cash or even swipe a card—charges simply happen in the background. The less friction there is, the less likely you are to notice, and the easier it becomes for companies to slip past your mental defenses.

The "Latte Factor" Debate—And the Hidden Truth

You've probably heard the classic personal finance advice: "Skip the daily latte and you'll save thousands over time." While catchy, this advice misses the point. Most people don't overspend because of one predictable habit like coffee. They overspend because of dozens of *unpredictable* small charges they don't track—subscription trials that never ended, fees buried in contracts, tiny bill increases that sneak by.

The danger isn't in your daily treat—it's in the expenses you don't consciously choose. The latte at least gives you joy. The unused $12 subscription gives you nothing.

How Companies Exploit the Psychology

Businesses design their pricing models to take advantage of our blind spots. Instead of charging $120 once, they charge $9.99 monthly. Instead of showing a total cost, they break it into "service fees," "convenience fees," and "processing fees," each small enough to seem harmless.

Streaming platforms, fitness apps, and even credit card companies know that people rarely cancel small recurring charges because they don't feel urgent. Behavioral economists call this *"status quo bias"*: the tendency to stick with what's already happening, even if it costs more over time.

Why AI Is Built for This Problem

The human brain isn't wired to monitor dozens of micro-charges across multiple accounts. You forget, you rationalize, and you move on. AI doesn't. It can scan every transaction, flag unusual patterns, and highlight charges you've stopped benefiting from. Instead of relying on memory or willpower, you let technology do what it does best: spot the invisible.

Imagine having a digital watchdog that never sleeps. Every time a small leak appears, it barks—not weeks later, but in real time. That's the role AI plays in transforming "death by a thousand cuts" into quick, painless savings.

Takeaway: Small charges don't feel dangerous, but they are the silent killers of financial health. They exploit natural blind spots in human psychology and thrive on being unnoticed. By shifting monitoring from human effort to AI automation, you finally gain the ability to see—and stop—the leaks that quietly drain your wallet.

How Companies Design Billing to Keep You Trapped

If you've ever tried to cancel a subscription or wondered why your bill quietly went up, it wasn't an accident—it was strategy. Companies across industries deliberately design billing systems to maximize revenue by keeping you paying as long as possible. This isn't about "bad customer service" or "oversight." It's a multi-billion-dollar science known as *behavioral design*.

The Free Trial Trap

Free trials are rarely "free." They're structured to convert into paying customers by exploiting inertia. Companies know that most people won't remember to cancel before the trial ends. That's why cancellation deadlines are often hidden in fine print and reminders conveniently forgotten.

One study showed that nearly **48% of people stay subscribed to a service after a free trial ends**, not because they love it, but because they forgot or couldn't figure out how to cancel. Every month after that is pure profit for the company.

The Complexity Game

Another tactic is what economists call *"sludge"*: making processes unnecessarily difficult so you give up. Signing up for a subscription takes 30 seconds; canceling it might take 30 minutes, with hidden menus, long wait times, or repeated "are you sure?" screens.

For example, some gym memberships require in-person cancellation with a written notice—an intentional barrier that banks on your procrastination. The harder it is to leave, the longer you stay—and the more you pay.

The Illusion of Small Numbers

Pricing strategies are also designed to trick the brain. $9.99 feels dramatically cheaper than $10, even though the difference is one cent. Breaking annual costs into monthly charges makes them look smaller. A $240 expense feels easier to accept when presented as "just $20 a month."

This tactic keeps you subscribed to services you wouldn't accept if you saw the full annual cost upfront. Companies are essentially banking on your short-term focus and underestimating long-term accumulation.

The Silent Price Creep

Many service providers—cable, internet, insurance—rely on what's known as "drip pricing." They start you with a promotional rate, then gradually increase the cost over time. Because each increase is small ($5 here, $7 there), most people don't bother to call and negotiate. Over years, this compounds into hundreds or thousands of dollars in overpayment.

Telecom companies, for instance, earn billions annually from this strategy. They know most customers don't track last year's bill against this year's. They also know customer inertia is strong: people will complain about rising costs but rarely switch providers.

Why This Works on You

These tactics succeed because they exploit deep human tendencies:

- **Inertia:** Once something is set up, we resist changing it.
- **Loss aversion:** We fear the "hassle" of canceling more than the ongoing cost.
- **Time scarcity:** We're too busy to notice—or fight—small billing changes.

Companies don't need to trick millions of people into big decisions. They only need to let millions of people *not notice small ones.*

Takeaway: Billing systems are not neutral—they're designed to trap you. From free trials that turn into hidden costs, to sludge-filled cancellation processes, to slow, silent price hikes, businesses thrive on your inattention. Once you recognize these tactics, you'll see why AI is essential: it cuts through the sludge, tracks the price creep, and helps you escape the traps that were built to keep you paying.

The Role of AI in Uncovering Invisible Patterns

Humans are not wired to track dozens of small, scattered charges across multiple accounts. Bills arrive at different times, subscriptions renew silently, and fees appear in confusing language. Even the most disciplined budgeter eventually misses something. This is where Artificial Intelligence changes the game: it doesn't just record transactions—it finds patterns you would never see on your own.

Pattern Recognition Beyond Human Capacity

AI thrives on analyzing vast amounts of data quickly. Where you might glance at a few statements each month, AI can scan years of financial history in seconds. It can group transactions, detect recurring charges, and identify anomalies that slip past the naked eye.

For example:

- You may notice your phone bill went up this month. AI notices it went up *every April for the past three years.*
- You may know you're subscribed to three streaming platforms. AI sees that two of them overlap by 90% in content you never watch.

- You may catch one overdraft fee. AI spots that your bank has charged you twelve of them in the last two years, totaling hundreds of dollars.

Patterns like these are invisible to memory and manual tracking—but obvious to an algorithm.

Turning Chaos Into Clarity

Financial statements are designed to confuse. A gym membership might appear as "FITLIFE-BILLING LLC," while a software subscription shows up as "XYZ SERVICES." To you, these are meaningless codes. To AI, they are instantly recognizable as recurring charges.

By translating raw transaction data into human-readable insights, AI strips away the fog companies rely on to keep you in the dark. Instead of a jumble of cryptic charges, you get a simple statement: *"You're paying $42 this month for three subscriptions you haven't used in 90 days."*

Predicting Future Leaks

AI doesn't stop at spotting the past. It can forecast future leaks before they happen. By analyzing trends, it can alert you when a "promotional rate" is set to expire, or when your spending is trending toward an overdraft. It can even simulate scenarios—like showing how much you'll save if you cancel one subscription or switch an insurance plan.

In other words, AI shifts you from reacting to problems to preventing them.

From Data to Action

The real power of AI isn't just analysis—it's automation. Once a pattern is uncovered, AI can suggest or even execute solutions. Cancel a duplicate subscription. Dispute an unfair fee. Draft a negotiation message to your internet provider.

Instead of staring at a spreadsheet that tells you what went wrong, you have a system that actively fixes what's wrong.

Takeaway: Companies rely on complexity to hide money leaks, but AI is built to see through the noise. By uncovering invisible patterns, predicting future traps, and automating fixes, AI turns financial confusion into clarity—and passive losses into active savings.

Checklist: 5 Places You're Almost Certainly Overspending

By now, you've seen how psychology and billing design combine to drain money without you noticing. But where, exactly, should you look first? Research shows that most households overspend in the same handful of areas. Think of this checklist as a flashlight: shine it on your finances and you'll almost certainly uncover hidden leaks.

1. Subscriptions You Don't Use

Streaming services, music apps, fitness platforms, cloud storage, and "free trial" apps that never got canceled. The average person pays for **7–10 subscriptions** but actively uses fewer than half. Even if each one costs only $10–$15, that's easily **$200–$400 a year** in wasted money.

AI fix: Tools can scan your email and bank records, list all active subscriptions, and flag duplicates or those you haven't logged into for months.

2. Internet, Phone, and Cable Bills

Service providers excel at "price creep." They lure you with promotional rates, then raise the price slowly, betting you won't notice. A $5–$10 hike per year doesn't trigger alarm bells, but over three years, you may be paying 30% more for the same service.

AI fix: Set up alerts that notify you the moment a bill changes. Some AI apps can even auto-chat with your provider to negotiate a lower rate.

---

3. Bank and Credit Card Fees

Overdraft charges, ATM fees, annual credit card fees, and late-payment penalties add up faster than most people realize. U.S. consumers paid **over $30 billion in overdraft fees alone last year**. Much of this comes from lack of awareness—not lack of money.

AI fix: AI-powered financial assistants can flag fees the moment they hit and, in some cases, automatically dispute them with the bank.

---

4. Insurance Premiums

Insurance companies reward new customers with discounts and quietly raise rates on loyal ones. Staying with the same provider for years often costs you hundreds more annually. Many people don't realize they're overpaying because premiums rise gradually.

AI fix: AI comparison tools can scan the market and show you equivalent coverage for less. A simple switch can save **$200–$500 a year**—without reducing protection.

5. Everyday Shopping Traps

Dynamic pricing means the same product can cost different people different amounts, depending on timing, browsing history, and location. Add in hidden delivery fees, unused coupons, and retail "upsells," and you're paying more than you should.

AI fix: Smart shopping extensions can automatically find lower prices, apply coupons, or activate cashback without you lifting a finger.

Your Action Step

Go through this checklist and identify which areas apply to you. Chances are, at least **three of the five** are quietly draining money from your account right now. Don't try to fix everything manually—this is exactly the kind of repetitive, detail-heavy work that AI is built to handle.

Takeaway: Most overspending doesn't come from bad decisions—it comes from invisible leaks hiding in plain sight. By focusing on these five areas and letting AI do the heavy lifting, you can reclaim hundreds (or even thousands) each year without cutting back on the things you actually enjoy.

CHAPTER 2

Subscription Overload: How to Stop Paying for What You Don't Use

AI Tools That Scan Bank and Email for Recurring Payments

The average consumer now juggles **7 to 10 active subscriptions**, from streaming and music platforms to meal kits, apps, and digital storage. Most people don't even remember signing up for half of them. Why? Because subscriptions are designed to blend into the background: small monthly charges that hit automatically, never demanding attention.

AI offers a new way to fight back—not by asking you to comb through statements manually, but by scanning your financial and digital footprint to identify recurring charges instantly.

Why Manual Tracking Doesn't Work

Imagine flipping through 12 months of bank statements trying to spot duplicate or unused services. It's time-consuming, error-prone, and—let's be honest—you're not going to do it. Companies know this, which is why they rely on *invisibility* as their most effective retention strategy.

Even if you catch one or two charges, you'll likely miss others hidden under confusing labels. A video subscription might show up as "STREAMCO MEDIA LLC." A fitness app could appear as "FITPAY SERVICES." Unless you have perfect recall for every sign-up you've ever made, some will slip through.

How AI Scanning Works

AI tools connect securely to your bank account, credit card, and sometimes even your email inbox (with permission). Instead of just listing every transaction, they use algorithms to detect repeating patterns: weekly, monthly, or annual charges.

Here's what that looks like in practice:

- You link your accounts to an AI-powered app.
- The app scans your transactions for recurring payments.
- It then generates a clear list: *"You are paying $13.99 for Disney+, $9.99 for Spotify, $49.99 annually for Dropbox."*
- It flags overlaps: *"You're paying for two music services— Spotify and Apple Music—totaling $240 per year."*

Suddenly, what was hidden becomes obvious.

The Power of Email Scans

Some AI tools also search your email for digital receipts and renewal notices. This matters because many subscriptions don't even hit your bank until the trial converts. By scanning confirmation emails, AI can warn you: *"This free trial will become a $14.99 monthly charge in 3 days."*

Instead of being surprised by an unwanted bill, you have time to cancel before it hits.

From Awareness to Action

The real value isn't just seeing what you're paying—it's acting on it. Many AI apps now include a **one-click cancel** option, saving you from the endless "log in, find settings, click through five screens" dance. Some even offer concierge-style services, where the app's team will cancel on your behalf.

This is crucial, because awareness alone rarely changes behavior. You might see that you're paying for three streaming services, but without an easy off-ramp, you'll procrastinate. AI removes the friction.

Takeaway: Subscriptions are built to be forgotten. AI scanning flips the power dynamic by exposing hidden charges, predicting upcoming renewals, and even canceling unused services for you. Instead of letting companies profit from your forgetfulness, you put technology in charge of remembering—so you don't have to.

Identifying Duplicate or Unused Subscriptions

When subscriptions first became popular, they felt liberating. For a small monthly fee, you got unlimited movies, music, or services. But over time, what started as convenience has turned into clutter. Millions of people now pay for subscriptions they don't use—or worse, multiple subscriptions that serve the same purpose.

The Duplicate Trap

Think about entertainment alone: Netflix, Hulu, Disney+, Amazon Prime Video, Apple TV, and countless niche platforms. Most people subscribe to at least three, but realistically, they only watch one or two consistently. The rest run quietly in the background, siphoning money.

The same happens with music services (Spotify *and* Apple Music), cloud storage (Google Drive *and* Dropbox), or fitness apps. Duplicates creep in when you sign up during promotions, bundle deals, or free trials that roll into paid plans.

Each one looks harmless at $9.99 a month, but duplicates can easily add up to **$300–$600 per year** in wasted money.

The "Set and Forget" Problem

Unused subscriptions are even more common. A fitness app you used for two weeks. An educational platform you promised to revisit. A meditation app that auto-renewed. Once the excitement wears off, these services fade into the background. But because they renew automatically, they keep charging you for months—or even years.

Research shows that the average consumer underestimates subscription spending by **nearly 200%**. In surveys, people often guess they're paying $80 a month, but in reality, it's closer to $200 or more. That gap comes from services they forgot exist.

How AI Spots Waste You Can't See

Identifying duplicates and unused subscriptions manually is nearly impossible—you'd need to track logins, usage, and spending across multiple platforms. AI can do this instantly by analyzing patterns such as:

- **Redundancy:** Paying for two or more services that deliver the same benefit.
- **Inactivity:** Subscriptions you haven't logged into for months.
- **Low value:** Services costing more than your actual usage justifies.

For example, AI might flag: *"You're paying $19.99 monthly for a premium music service, but you've streamed less than 10 songs in the last 90 days."* That's a nudge most people need to cut the cord.

From Guilt to Empowerment

The key isn't to cancel everything—it's to keep only what truly adds value. Maybe Netflix is worth it because you watch it every week. But if you're holding onto two other platforms "just in case," that's money leaking for no reason.

AI helps you make these choices without guilt. Instead of guessing, you see the numbers. Instead of procrastinating, you cancel with one click. The decision becomes less emotional and more factual.

Takeaway: Duplicate and unused subscriptions are the low-hanging fruit of financial leaks—easy to miss, but even easier to fix once you see them. AI exposes these hidden costs and gives you the power to cut them quickly, keeping only what you actually use and value.

Beating the "Free Trial" Trap Before It Hits Your Card

Few marketing strategies are more powerful than the "free trial." You get 7, 14, or 30 days of access with no upfront payment—just enter your credit card "for verification." Companies know most people won't cancel on time, and that's exactly the point. What feels like generosity is really a calculated bet: if they hook you with frictionless sign-up and high-friction cancellation, they'll win recurring revenue without you noticing.

Why Free Trials Work Against You

The trap works because of three psychological triggers:

1. **Optimism Bias:** You believe you'll remember to cancel before the trial ends. But life gets busy, and the deadline passes unnoticed.
2. **Inertia:** Once the subscription converts to paid, you think, "I'll cancel later." Later rarely comes.
3. **Loss Aversion:** After trying the service, you may fear missing out—even if you barely used it. That "what if I need it?" thought keeps you paying.

One study found that more than **50% of people forget to cancel free trials on time**, and many continue paying for months afterward.

The Business Model of Forgetfulness

Companies design trials with this forgetfulness in mind. That's why:

- Cancellation instructions are buried in account settings.
- Trials end on weekends or holidays when you're less likely to notice.
- Reminders are vague or absent altogether.

Some even extend the strategy by offering a low-priced "introductory month" after the trial, hoping to blend charges into your regular spending.

How AI Defends Against Trial Traps

AI tools can track your free trials automatically. By scanning your email inbox for "trial confirmation" messages and your bank account for upcoming renewals, they create a timeline of when each trial will convert into a paid plan.

Here's how it works in practice:

- You sign up for a free trial.
- The AI logs the start date, length of trial, and renewal cost.
- Three days before the trial ends, you get an alert: *"Your Audible trial will renew at $14.95/month. Cancel now to avoid the charge."*
- In some cases, the AI can even **cancel the trial for you** with one click.

This shifts the dynamic from passive risk to active prevention. Instead of being surprised by a bill, you're reminded in time to make a choice.

Turning Free Trials Into True Free Trials

Free trials don't have to be bad. They're a chance to test services risk-free—as long as you maintain control. With AI as your safety net, you can actually use the trial period for its intended purpose: evaluate whether the service adds real value. If it doesn't, you exit cleanly without paying a cent.

Takeaway: Free trials aren't designed to give you something for free—they're designed to lock you in. But with AI tracking renewal dates and auto-canceling unwanted trials, you flip the script. Companies no longer profit from your forgetfulness, and you reclaim the freedom to test services on your own terms.

Template: Email/Script to Cancel a Stubborn Service

Some companies make cancellation easy. Others bury you in endless menus, long wait times, or customer service agents trained to keep you paying. This isn't by accident—it's called *"retention strategy"*, and the goal is to make leaving so frustrating that you give up.

That's why it helps to have a ready-made script: clear, professional, and firm. Below is a template you can adapt for email, chat, or phone.

Email/Chat Cancellation Template

Subject: Request to Cancel Subscription – [Your Name / Account Number]

Hello [Company Name] Support Team,

I am writing to request the immediate cancellation of my subscription with [Company Name], linked to [your email/account ID].

Please confirm the following in writing:

1. My subscription has been canceled effective immediately.
2. No further charges will be billed to my account.
3. A confirmation of the final billing date and any applicable refunds.

I expect this request to be honored without delay, as per consumer protection guidelines. Please send me written confirmation within 48 hours.

Thank you,
[Your Full Name]
[Your Contact Information]

Phone Script for Customer Service

When you call, expect the agent to try to "save" your account with discounts or offers. Stay polite, but firm.

You: Hello, I'd like to cancel my subscription effective today. My account is under [your name/email].

Agent: Can I ask why you're canceling? We can offer you a discount.

You: I appreciate the offer, but my decision is final. Please cancel my account and send me a confirmation email.

Agent: Are you sure? We can pause your subscription instead.

You: Thank you, but I am not interested in alternatives. Please proceed with the cancellation and confirm that no further charges will occur.

Repeat calmly until they agree. The key is to use short, clear sentences—no explanations, no justifications.

AI Can Do This For You

Some AI money-saving tools already automate this process. Instead of sending the email or making the call yourself, you authorize the AI's cancellation service, and they handle the negotiation on your behalf. This eliminates the stress of back-and-forth conversations designed to wear you down.

Takeaway: Canceling shouldn't feel like a battle—but many companies design it that way. Having a ready-to-use script makes the process faster, firmer, and less emotional. And with AI increasingly taking on this task, you may never have to argue with a retention agent again.

CHAPTER 3

Bill Creep: Why Internet, Phone, and Utilities Always Rise

How Service Providers Quietly Increase Rates

Every year, millions of customers notice their internet, phone, or utility bills creeping upward. Sometimes it's only a few dollars. Other times it's masked under "new fees" or "updated service charges." Rarely does anyone receive a clear explanation. This steady rise is not random—it's a deliberate strategy built on the assumption that most people won't notice, and even fewer will take action.

The Promotional Rate Trap

Most providers lure customers in with a low "introductory" price. Internet at $49.99 a month sounds like a great deal—until you realize that rate expires after 12 months. Without warning, the bill jumps to $69.99 or $79.99. Buried somewhere in the contract was a clause about the increase, but it was likely phrased in fine print designed to be ignored.

This is one of the oldest tricks in the book: attract new customers with a bargain, then quietly shift them into a higher-paying tier once inertia kicks in.

The Drip Pricing Strategy

Instead of one big increase that customers might fight, companies often raise prices in small increments. A $5 hike here, a $3 "network maintenance fee" there. Individually, these changes feel too minor to spend an hour on the phone disputing. But over time, they compound.

Take an internet plan that starts at $60/month. Add $5 increases for three consecutive years, and you're suddenly paying $75 for the same service—an extra $180 annually. Multiply that across millions of customers, and providers pocket billions from this tactic alone.

Hidden Fees Disguised as Necessities

Another common trick is the introduction of "regulatory recovery fees," "service maintenance charges," or "convenience fees." These sound official—sometimes even like government-imposed taxes. In reality, they're often just revenue boosters invented by the company. Because the wording suggests legitimacy, most customers don't question them.

One telecom giant was found to have earned over **$1 billion annually** from vaguely named fees that had no direct service value. Customers saw them as unavoidable, when in fact they were optional add-ons disguised as requirements.

Banking on Customer Inertia

Why do providers get away with this? Because they know most people won't switch. Canceling internet or phone service is inconvenient, requires time on hold, and often involves equipment returns or activation fees with a new company. Providers leverage this friction. They understand that even if customers grumble, 90% will pay rather than go through the hassle of changing providers.

Behavioral economists call this *status quo bias*: the tendency to stick with the current option, even if it's worse, simply because change feels difficult. Service providers have turned that bias into a business model.

The Psychology of "It's Just a Few Dollars"

Companies don't need you to accept a $20 hike—they just need you to accept $3–$5 hikes repeatedly. Most customers think, *"It's only a few bucks, not worth the fight."* But add that up across internet, phone, utilities, and insurance, and you're losing **hundreds of dollars every year**—not because of one big mistake, but because of dozens of tiny, unnoticed ones.

Takeaway: Service providers quietly increase rates through promotional traps, drip pricing, hidden fees, and by exploiting customer inertia. They count on you being too busy—or too tired—to fight back. Recognizing these tactics is the first step toward stopping the slow bleed of "bill creep" that eats away at your budget every year.

Setting AI Alerts for Bill Hikes

The biggest problem with "bill creep" isn't the increase itself—it's how quietly it happens. A $5 or $10 hike can slip by unnoticed in the blur of monthly charges, and by the time you realize it, you've already paid extra for months. The solution isn't obsessively checking every bill. It's automating the process with AI alerts that act as watchdogs on your behalf.

Why Manual Tracking Fails

Think about your internet or utility bill. Do you remember what you paid six months ago? Probably not. Service providers count on that forgetfulness. Even if you're diligent about reviewing bills, charges are often buried in confusing layouts: new fees tucked into fine print, totals rounded up with taxes, or "package adjustments" that make comparisons difficult.

Human attention is limited. AI attention is not.

How AI Alerts Work

When you connect your accounts to an AI-powered money tool, it doesn't just log transactions—it tracks patterns over time. Here's what happens behind the scenes:

1. **Baseline established:** The AI records your typical monthly bill (e.g., internet at $69.99).
2. **Continuous monitoring:** Each new bill is compared against the baseline.

3. **Instant alert:** If the charge jumps unexpectedly—say from $69.99 to $79.99—you receive a notification immediately.

Some tools even break down *why* the bill increased, distinguishing between legitimate taxes and manufactured fees.

From Alert to Action

An alert alone is useful, but the real value comes in what you do next. Many AI tools now include built-in responses such as:

- **Drafting a negotiation message** to your provider.
- **Offering cancellation options** for overpriced services.
- **Highlighting cheaper competitors** so you can switch with confidence.

Instead of just knowing your bill went up, you're handed a solution within minutes.

Proactive Protection vs. Passive Discovery

Traditionally, most people only notice rate hikes after months of overpaying. AI flips this dynamic by turning bill management from reactive to proactive. You're not playing catch-up—you're intercepting the problem before it becomes expensive.

For example:

- Without AI: You discover in December that your utility bill has been $15 higher since July—$90 already gone.
- With AI: You're alerted in July, dispute the charge, and prevent the extra $90 loss.

The Peace of Automation

The true benefit of AI alerts is psychological. You no longer need to live with the low-level anxiety of "I wonder if my bills went up." The monitoring happens automatically, giving you peace of mind and freeing up mental bandwidth for more important things than chasing pennies on statements.

Takeaway: Bill creep thrives on your inattention. By setting AI alerts, you gain a digital watchdog that notices every increase, explains the reason, and arms you with solutions. Instead of letting companies quietly take more, you stay in control—without lifting a finger.

Negotiating Like a Pro (AI Scripts + Chatbot Hacks)

If you've ever tried to negotiate a lower bill, you know how frustrating it can be: long hold times, agents trained to push back, and endless back-and-forth that leaves you drained. Companies design this experience deliberately—making it so unpleasant that most people simply give up. But here's the secret: negotiation works. The problem isn't *whether* providers will lower your bill—it's whether you're willing to fight through the process. That's where AI comes in.

Why Negotiation Matters

Service providers build "wiggle room" into their pricing models. They expect a small percentage of customers to push back, so they budget for discounts, promotions, or loyalty credits. If you don't ask, you pay the inflated price. If you do ask, you often win.

Surveys show that **over 80% of customers who negotiate their internet or cable bill receive a discount**, yet less than 30% attempt it. In other words, companies are profiting from silence.

How AI Scripts Change the Game

AI can draft tailored negotiation messages in seconds—firm, polite, and backed by data. Instead of fumbling for words, you copy and paste a script that makes you sound like a professional negotiator. For example:

Sample AI-Generated Script (Chat or Email):

"Hello, I've noticed that my monthly bill for [service] has increased from $X to $Y. I'd like to remain a loyal customer, but at this rate I will need to consider switching providers. Could you review my account for any available promotions, loyalty discounts, or rate adjustments? I'm looking for a solution that keeps my monthly bill consistent with the market."

Short, polite, and to the point. This kind of message often unlocks hidden discounts that agents won't offer unless pressed.

Chatbot Hacks: Beating Providers at Their Own Game

Many providers now use chatbots to handle support requests. Most customers get frustrated, but AI-savvy users see this as an advantage. With the right phrasing, you can unlock human-agent intervention faster, or trigger the chatbot to offer discounts automatically.

Pro Hacks:

- Use keywords like *"cancel service"* early. Companies are trained to fight hard when they sense you're leaving. Often, this triggers retention discounts.
- Ask: *"Can you match competitor pricing?"* Chatbots are often programmed to offer immediate adjustments rather than escalate.
- Keep your tone firm but polite. Chat systems flag aggressive language and may shut down requests.

AI-Assisted Negotiation Tools

Some AI-powered services go beyond scripts—they'll actually **negotiate for you.** By connecting your accounts, the AI system contacts your provider, argues on your behalf, and applies savings automatically. Customers have reported discounts of **10–30% off bills** with zero direct effort.

Imagine never sitting on hold again, while still reaping the benefits of lower rates.

Why This Works Consistently

Companies spend millions acquiring new customers. Retaining an existing one, even at a lower rate, is almost always cheaper for them. That's why negotiation works more often than not—it's about economics, not charity. AI simply removes the friction that prevents most people from asking in the first place.

Takeaway: Negotiating bills doesn't require hours of frustration anymore. With AI scripts and chatbot hacks, you can approach providers with confidence—or let automation handle it entirely. The result? Lower bills, less stress, and hundreds of dollars back in your pocket each year.

Case Study: $480 Saved in 20 Minutes

Sometimes the best way to understand the power of fighting bill creep is to see it in action. Here's a real-world example of how one customer turned a creeping internet bill into almost five hundred dollars in savings—with less than half an hour of effort.

The Situation

Maria, a freelance designer, noticed her internet bill had jumped from $69.99 to $84.99 over the past year. At first, she ignored it. "It's just $15," she thought. But when an AI money tool flagged the increase, she realized she'd already spent **$180 extra in a single year**—and the provider was likely to raise it again.

Step 1: AI Alert + Script

Her AI assistant sent her an alert: *"Your internet bill increased by $15. Would you like to request a rate adjustment?"* It also generated a negotiation script she could copy into the provider's live chat.

The script was short and professional:

"Hello, I've noticed my monthly bill has increased from $69.99 to $84.99. I'd like to stay with your service, but at this price I'll need to consider switching providers. Could you review my account for loyalty discounts or promotions?"

Step 2: The Chatbot Dance

Within two minutes, a chatbot responded with a generic apology and an offer to "review the account." Maria stayed calm and copied another AI-generated follow-up:

"I'm looking for options that keep my bill consistent with the market. Can you match competitor pricing?"

The chatbot escalated her to a human agent.

Step 3: The Retention Offer

The agent quickly offered a "limited-time loyalty discount" that reduced her bill back to $69.99—and added three months at $59.99. Total savings over the next 12 months: **$240.**

But Maria wasn't done. Her AI assistant suggested one more push: *"Can you check for additional bundles or credits for long-term customers?"*

After a pause, the agent applied a $20 credit to her account, plus locked in the lower rate for two years instead of one.

The Result

By the end of a **20-minute chat**, Maria had saved **$480 over the next two years**—without raising her voice, making phone calls, or memorizing negotiation tactics. The AI did the heavy lifting: spotting the increase, drafting the language, and guiding her step by step.

Why This Matters

Maria's story isn't unusual. Providers expect most people to stay silent, so those who push back—especially with the right language—almost always get results. The difference is that Maria didn't have to rely on willpower or negotiation skills. AI turned a frustrating task into a quick, nearly effortless win.

Takeaway: Bill creep can cost you hundreds before you even notice. But with AI alerts, scripts, and a little persistence, you can reverse the creep in minutes. Maria's $480 win proves the point: small actions, guided by smart tools, can deliver outsized savings.

CHAPTER 4

Bank Fees, Credit Card Traps, and Hidden Charges

The Most Common Fees Banks Don't Want You to Notice

Banks and credit card companies don't just make money from interest and lending—they make billions each year from fees so small and hidden that most customers never notice them. Unlike a one-time big charge, these fees are designed to be subtle, recurring, and psychologically easy to ignore. Yet for the average household, they quietly add up to hundreds of dollars annually.

Overdraft Fees: The Big Profit Machine

Overdraft fees are one of the most infamous bank charges. When your account balance dips below zero, even for a few hours, the bank may cover the payment—but they'll charge you $35 or more for the "service."

Here's the catch:

- Many banks process the *largest* transactions first (like rent), draining your account faster, so smaller charges that follow trigger multiple overdrafts.
- Even if you deposit money the same day, the fee often sticks.

In 2022 alone, U.S. banks collected over **$8 billion in overdraft fees**, a revenue stream built almost entirely on customer mistakes.

ATM Fees: Paying to Access Your Own Money

Using an out-of-network ATM may seem like a small inconvenience, but it often costs $3–$5 per withdrawal. If you're traveling or in a hurry, these fees can stack up quickly. Worse, you're usually paying **two fees at once**: one to your bank, and one to the ATM operator.

Make that mistake just twice a month, and you're losing $120 annually—for nothing more than convenience.

Credit Card Late Fees

Miss a due date by even a single day, and your credit card issuer may charge $25–$40. Repeat the mistake within six months, and the fee can jump higher. Not only does this waste money, but it can also increase your interest rates and damage your credit score—costing you far more in the long run.

Hidden Maintenance and "Service" Fees

Some banks still charge "monthly maintenance" fees just to keep your account open. These fees often hit accounts that fall below a minimum balance, trapping customers with lower incomes.

Then there are obscure charges like "statement fees" (for mailed paper statements), "inactivity fees" (for accounts you don't use), or "foreign transaction fees" (often 2–3% on international purchases). Each is designed to look minor, but together they quietly erode your balance.

Why We Don't Notice

The psychology of fees is deliberate:

- They're small enough to avoid outrage.
- They're buried in long statements or vague line items.
- They're tied to "policies" that sound official, making you assume they're unavoidable.

In reality, most fees are highly negotiable—or preventable once you're aware of them. But banks and credit card companies profit from the fact that most people never question them.

Takeaway: Bank and credit card fees are not random—they're engineered revenue streams built on consumer inattention. Overdrafts, ATM surcharges, late fees, and "maintenance" charges may seem small in isolation, but together they drain billions from customers each year. The good news? With AI tools and the right strategies, you can stop paying for mistakes and start keeping your money where it belongs—in your account.

AI That Auto-Flags and Disputes Charges

Banks and credit card companies rely on one thing: you not noticing. A $35 overdraft fee, a $4 ATM surcharge, or a $15 "maintenance" charge blends into the noise of dozens of monthly transactions. But what if you had a digital assistant that never blinked, never forgot, and challenged every unfair charge the moment it appeared? That's exactly what AI can do.

Why Manual Monitoring Fails

In theory, you could catch these fees yourself by reviewing every statement line by line. In reality, few people have the time—or the mental energy—to audit hundreds of small transactions every month. And even if you spot a fee, disputing it requires calling customer service, waiting on hold, and explaining your case. Most people simply let it slide.

That's the business model: profit from silence.

How AI Flags Fees Instantly

AI-powered financial tools connect securely to your accounts and analyze every transaction in real time. They're trained to recognize the language banks use to disguise fees—terms like *"overdraft item," "NSF charge," "monthly service,"* or *"foreign transaction."*

When a suspicious fee appears, you get an alert:

- *"A $35 overdraft fee was charged on your checking account today."*
- *"Your credit card statement includes a $29 late fee. Want to dispute?"*

Instead of discovering the loss weeks later, you know immediately.

Disputing Without the Headache

Here's where AI takes it further. Some tools now offer **one-click dispute options.** Tap a button, and the system automatically drafts a professional, legally grounded message to your bank or credit card company.

For example:

"I am disputing the overdraft fee charged on [date]. I request a courtesy waiver as a loyal customer and ask that the charge be reversed."

Because banks often budget for "goodwill credits," these disputes are surprisingly effective. In fact, studies show that **over 40% of disputed bank fees are refunded**—but only if the customer asks. AI makes sure you always ask.

Case in Point

One popular AI-powered app reported saving users **over $1 billion in bank fees** by automatically detecting and disputing charges. Many users had no idea they were being drained until the app intervened.

For example, a customer who had been paying a $15 monthly "service fee" for over a year received an alert—and a full refund of

$180—after AI flagged the charge and sent a dispute message on their behalf.

A Watchdog That Never Sleeps

The real power of AI isn't just catching a single mistake—it's persistent vigilance. Every transaction is monitored, every fee questioned, every unfair charge challenged. It's like having a lawyer read every line of your statement 24/7, but without the hourly rate.

Takeaway: Banks and credit card companies profit from unnoticed fees and customer inaction. AI flips the script by spotting charges instantly and disputing them automatically. What once felt like a tedious battle becomes a background process that keeps money in your pocket—with almost no effort from you.

Protecting Your Credit Score While Cutting Costs

Saving money on fees and charges is powerful—but not if it accidentally damages your credit score in the process. Many people avoid negotiating bills or disputing charges because they fear it will somehow "look bad" to lenders. Others cut costs so aggressively (like closing accounts or canceling cards) that they unknowingly hurt their own financial reputation. The key is balance: reducing costs while keeping your credit score strong.

Why Your Credit Score Matters

Your credit score isn't just about getting loans. It affects:

- **Interest rates:** A higher score can save you thousands on mortgages, car loans, or credit cards.
- **Insurance premiums:** Many insurers use credit scores to set rates.

- **Housing opportunities:** Landlords often run credit checks before approving rentals.
- **Job prospects:** Some employers review credit history for roles requiring financial responsibility.

A few missteps—like closing the wrong account or letting a small bill go unpaid—can have ripple effects far beyond a $30 fee.

Smart Moves vs. Costly Mistakes

Smart Cost-Cutting Moves:

- **Disputing fees:** Challenging unfair charges does *not* harm your credit score. If anything, it protects your record from showing unnecessary late payments.
- **Negotiating lower interest rates:** Calling your credit card company and requesting a reduced APR can save you hundreds in interest without any negative effect.
- **Setting AI reminders:** Late payments are the single biggest factor in credit score damage. AI tools that nudge you before due dates help you stay flawless.

Costly Mistakes to Avoid:

- **Closing old credit cards:** Even if you don't use a card often, closing it can shorten your credit history and raise your utilization ratio—both harmful to your score.
- **Paying bills late while disputing:** Always pay at least the minimum due while a dispute is pending. Otherwise, the bank may report you as late even if you win the argument later.
- **Overusing credit lines:** Cutting costs doesn't mean maxing out cheaper cards. Utilization above 30% can hurt your score, even if you pay in full each month.

How AI Protects Your Credit While Saving You Money

AI isn't just about finding leaks—it can also guard your credit health while you cut costs. Here's how:

- **Payment reminders:** AI tracks due dates across all accounts and alerts you days before, preventing accidental late payments.
- **Safe cancellation guidance:** Before you close an account, AI can warn you: *"Canceling this credit card may lower your score due to shorter account history."*
- **Automated minimum payments:** Some AI tools can auto-schedule small payments to keep accounts current while you negotiate or restructure balances.

This ensures you save money *today* without sacrificing financial stability *tomorrow*.

A Balanced Approach

Think of your finances like a ship: cutting costs is like patching leaks, but your credit score is the engine that drives you forward. You can't afford to save $100 today if it slows you down by thousands in the future. The smartest strategy is to let AI handle both: patching leaks while keeping the engine running smoothly.

Takeaway: Cutting costs shouldn't come at the expense of your credit score. By disputing fees strategically, keeping accounts healthy, and letting AI manage reminders and risks, you can enjoy savings today *and* protect the financial opportunities of tomorrow.

Template: Letter/Email to Dispute Unfair Fees

Disputing a fee can feel intimidating—but it doesn't have to be. Banks process millions of these requests each year, and many fees are reversed simply because the customer asked. The key is to be polite, precise, and firm. Below is a ready-to-use template you can adapt for overdraft charges, late fees, or other unfair bank or credit card charges.

Email/Letter Template

Subject: Request for Fee Reversal – [Your Name / Account Number]

Hello [Bank/Credit Card Company] Customer Service,

I am writing to formally dispute the [describe fee, e.g., $35 overdraft fee] charged to my account on [date].

I have been a loyal customer since [year], and this charge does not reflect my typical account activity. I respectfully request that this fee be waived as a courtesy.

Please confirm:

1. The removal of this charge from my account balance.
2. Written confirmation of the adjustment.

I value our relationship and appreciate your prompt attention to this matter.

Thank you,
[Your Full Name]
[Your Account Number]
[Your Contact Information]

Phone Script Variation

If you're calling instead of emailing, you can simplify:

"Hello, I'm calling about a [$XX] fee charged on my account on [date]. I'd like to request a courtesy waiver. I've been a customer since [year], and this fee doesn't reflect my usual activity. Can you remove it for me today?"

Stay polite but persistent. If the first representative says no, ask to speak with a supervisor. Banks often allow multiple fee reversals per year, but they rarely offer unless you request it.

AI Can Do This for You

Some AI-powered financial assistants now generate these letters automatically—or even send them for you. Instead of writing or calling, you simply approve the dispute, and the system handles the wording, timing, and follow-up. The result? Higher success rates with almost no effort on your part.

Takeaway: Banks expect silence, not pushback. A clear, respectful letter or script is often enough to get fees reversed—saving you money instantly. With AI tools generating and sending disputes automatically, this once-annoying task becomes as simple as clicking a button.

CHAPTER 5

Insurance Secrets: How to Stop Overpaying for Coverage

Why Loyalty Is Punished in Insurance Markets

We're taught from childhood that loyalty is a virtue. Stick with the same brand, the same provider, the same company—and you'll be rewarded. Unfortunately, the insurance industry works in the opposite way. Staying loyal doesn't earn you discounts. In fact, it often guarantees you'll pay **more** over time.

The "Loyalty Penalty"

Insurance companies use a pricing strategy called *price optimization.* Instead of rewarding long-term customers, they gradually increase rates for those least likely to shop around. If you've been with the same insurer for years, they assume you value convenience over savings. The result? You're quietly charged more than new customers for the same coverage.

A study in the U.K. found that loyal customers in home and auto insurance markets were paying **over 30% more** than new customers with identical risk profiles. Similar trends exist in the U.S., where insurers aggressively court new customers with "welcome rates" while slowly squeezing existing ones.

Why Loyalty Backfires

From the insurer's perspective, loyalty equals predictability. They know you won't bother comparing rates every year. Behavioral economists call this *status quo bias*—our tendency to stick with what we already have, even if it costs more. Insurers exploit this bias, raising your premium in small increments so the pain feels tolerable.

It's not unusual for someone who's been with the same auto insurer for 10 years to pay hundreds more annually than a new customer who signed up yesterday.

The "Teaser Rate" Game

Much like internet or phone providers, insurance companies lure new customers with teaser rates: deep discounts for the first year, followed by gradual increases. New sign-ups look like bargains, while long-time customers slowly absorb the true cost of staying.

Even worse, insurers often bundle products—auto, home, renters, life—to make switching feel overwhelming. Customers think, *"It's too much hassle to untangle everything,"* and end up staying, even as rates rise steadily.

How Loyalty Costs You

Let's say you pay $1,200 annually for car insurance. If your premium increases by 6% each year—a modest figure—that's $72 the first year, $147 the next, and $233 by year five. Over a decade, you've paid nearly **$1,500 extra** simply because you didn't shop around.

Multiply that across auto, home, renters, and health insurance, and the "loyalty penalty" easily reaches **thousands of dollars** over a lifetime.

Why AI Breaks the Cycle

The good news? Loyalty penalties only work if you don't notice them. AI changes the equation by tracking your premiums, comparing them against competitors, and alerting you when it's time to switch. Instead of assuming you'll stay silent, insurers face a customer armed with data and ready to act.

Takeaway: In insurance, loyalty isn't rewarded—it's exploited. Companies quietly raise premiums on long-term customers, banking on your inertia. By recognizing the "loyalty penalty" and using AI to monitor rates, you flip the power dynamic and stop paying more simply because you stayed put.

Using AI to Compare and Shop Policies

Comparing insurance policies has always been a headache. Dozens of providers, pages of fine print, and endless jargon about deductibles, exclusions, and "riders." It's no surprise that most people default to staying with their current insurer—even if it means overpaying year after year. But AI has completely changed the way consumers can shop for coverage. Instead of spending hours researching, you can now let technology do the heavy lifting and find the best policy for your needs in minutes.

Why Insurance Comparison Is So Hard

Insurance is designed to be confusing. Policies look similar on the surface but differ in critical details—like coverage limits or hidden exclusions. Price alone doesn't tell the whole story. Two policies at $100/month may provide radically different levels of protection.

Traditionally, you'd need to read through fine print, call agents, or use comparison websites that often prioritize companies paying for placement. This process is time-consuming, biased, and mentally exhausting.

How AI Simplifies the Process

AI-powered platforms cut through this complexity by analyzing thousands of policy options in seconds. Here's how they work:

1. **Input basics:** You provide details like your age, location, car/home type, or coverage needs.
2. **Automated scanning:** The AI searches multiple insurers, pulling real-time quotes.
3. **Contextual matching:** Instead of just showing price, it highlights trade-offs—like higher deductibles, better customer service scores, or faster claims processing.
4. **Personalized ranking:** The system recommends the best-value options tailored to your actual usage and risk profile.

In other words, AI does what you'd never have time (or patience) to do yourself.

Going Beyond Price

What sets AI apart from traditional comparison tools is its ability to look beyond the sticker price. For example, it can:

- Flag policies with hidden exclusions.
- Weigh customer satisfaction data from thousands of reviews.
- Predict long-term costs by factoring in likely premium increases.
- Match policy features to your actual habits—for example, recommending usage-based car insurance if you drive infrequently.

Instead of asking, *"Which is cheapest today?"* you start asking, *"Which will save me the most over time?"*

Real-World Example

Consider health insurance. Manually comparing options might mean flipping through 20 different plan brochures. An AI tool, however, can cross-check your actual medical spending over the past year, then recommend the plan that minimizes both premiums *and* out-of-pocket costs. That's not guesswork—that's data-driven precision.

Making Switching Easy

Comparison is only half the battle—switching is the part most people avoid. Some AI tools now streamline this too: they prepare cancellation letters, transfer documents, and even pre-fill forms for your new insurer. What used to feel like a mountain of paperwork becomes a five-minute process.

Takeaway: Insurance companies profit from complexity, hoping you'll stay put rather than shop around. AI breaks through the noise, comparing policies instantly, flagging hidden traps, and even handling the switch. The result? Better coverage at a lower cost—without the research marathon.

When to Switch — and When to Stay

Switching insurance providers can save you hundreds of dollars a year, but it's not always the right move. In some cases, staying put can actually be smarter—if you know how to play the system. The trick is understanding the signals that tell you whether it's time to move on or hold your ground.

When Switching Saves You Money

1. **Premium Hikes Without Added Value**
   If your rates have gone up significantly but your coverage hasn't improved, that's a red flag. AI tools can highlight these silent increases and compare them against market averages. If you're paying 15% more than the going rate, it's time to shop around.
2. **Better Deals for New Customers Elsewhere**
   Many insurers lure new clients with discounts—while raising prices for existing ones. If a competitor offers the same coverage at a lower rate, switching can put immediate money back in your pocket.
3. **Life Changes That Affect Risk**
   Moved to a safer neighborhood? Driving less than you used to? Paid off a car loan? These life changes can lower your risk profile, meaning you qualify for cheaper insurance. If your current provider doesn't adjust your premium, another one will.

4. **Bundling Opportunities**
   Sometimes switching lets you combine policies (auto +
   home, for example) for a discount. Just make sure the bundle
   truly saves money—AI can calculate whether the "deal" is
   real or just a marketing trick.

When Staying Is Smarter

1. **Loyalty Perks That Actually Pay Off**
   Not all loyalty is punished. Some companies reward long-
   term customers with accident forgiveness, free add-ons, or
   deeper coverage at the same rate. If the perks outweigh small
   premium hikes, staying may be the better choice.
2. **Short-Term Rate Stability**
   If you recently filed a claim, switching too soon could spike
   your premiums. Insurers often raise rates after claims, but
   your current provider might keep increases lower than
   competitors would. AI can simulate the impact of switching
   after a claim to show you the real cost.
3. **Customer Service and Claims Efficiency**
   Price isn't everything. A slightly higher premium may be
   worth it if your current insurer pays claims quickly and with
   less hassle. AI reviews can now measure customer
   satisfaction, giving you a clear picture of whether service
   quality justifies staying.

The Middle Ground: Renegotiating

Before you switch, always try renegotiating. With data from AI
comparisons, you can go to your current provider and say:

*"I've received a quote for the same coverage at $X. Can you match
or beat it?"*

Insurers know it's cheaper to retain you than to win a new customer,
so many will adjust your premium if they believe you're ready to
leave.

Takeaway: Switching insurance isn't about chasing the lowest number—it's about aligning cost, coverage, and service with your actual needs. AI helps you see the full picture, showing when switching is the smart play and when staying gives you the best long-term value.

Checklist: Insurance Optimization Routine (Annual)

Insurance isn't something you can "set and forget." Policies that seemed like a good deal last year may now be overpriced, outdated, or full of coverage you don't need. The good news is that keeping your insurance optimized doesn't require constant effort—just one focused check-up each year. Think of it as your financial health exam for insurance.

Here's a simple annual routine you can follow, powered by AI and a few smart habits:

1. Gather Your Current Policies

Collect your auto, home, renters, health, or life insurance documents. AI apps can often pull digital copies directly from your email or provider accounts, saving you the hassle of digging through paperwork.

Why it matters: You need a clear snapshot of your current premiums, deductibles, and coverage limits before you can compare.

---

2. Run an AI-Powered Comparison

Use an AI tool to scan the market for equivalent coverage. Look at least three alternatives for each major policy. Don't just compare price—pay attention to coverage gaps, claim ratings, and long-term cost predictions.

Why it matters: Most savings opportunities are invisible unless you line your policy up against competitors.

---

3. Flag Life Changes

Update your profile with any major changes: new car, safer neighborhood, fewer miles driven, home renovations, or paying off a loan. AI can calculate how these factors lower your risk—and therefore your premiums.

Why it matters: Insurers won't reduce your rate unless you ask.

4. Check for Duplicate or Unnecessary Coverage

Sometimes multiple policies overlap. For example, your credit card may already include rental car insurance, or your home insurance may already cover certain valuables. AI can detect redundancies and suggest cuts.

Why it matters: Over-insuring is just as costly as under-insuring.

---

5. Decide: Switch, Stay, or Renegotiate

Based on the data, make your move:

- **Switch** if another provider offers the same or better coverage for significantly less.
- **Stay** if your current provider matches competitor rates or offers perks worth the premium.

- **Renegotiate** by showing your provider competitor quotes and asking them to adjust.

Why it matters: The biggest mistake isn't overpaying—it's staying passive.

---

6. Automate Reminders for Next Year

Set a calendar alert—or let AI do it for you—to repeat this process annually. Even if you find no savings this year, rates shift constantly. Next year may unlock opportunities.

Your Annual Savings in Action

Running this optimization routine once a year typically saves households **$200–$500 per policy**—without reducing protection. Over a lifetime, that adds up to tens of thousands of dollars, simply by refusing to let insurers profit from your inertia.

Takeaway: Insurance optimization isn't about chasing the cheapest policy every year. It's about creating a repeatable system that ensures you always pay the right amount for the right coverage. With AI handling comparisons and reminders, this routine becomes almost effortless—while delivering lifelong savings.

CHAPTER 6

Everyday Spending Hacks with AI

How AI Finds Hidden Grocery/Retail Overpricing

For most households, groceries and everyday retail purchases are among the biggest recurring expenses. Unlike fixed bills, these costs feel flexible—yet they quietly swell with markups, hidden fees, and pricing tricks designed to make you spend more than you realize. What's worse, these overcharges are often so small and spread out that they fly under the radar. This is exactly where AI shines: it can spot patterns of overpricing that human shoppers simply don't have the time or memory to track.

The Invisible Markup Problem

When you walk into a grocery store or add items to an online cart, you assume the price is fair. But retailers often add subtle markups:

- **Delivery and convenience fees** that appear at checkout.
- **Package shrinkflation** (a "family size" cereal box that quietly lost two ounces but costs the same).
- **Store-by-store price differences** on identical items.

Individually, these differences look trivial. Over a year, they can add up to **hundreds of dollars in silent overspending.**

Why Humans Don't Catch It

Even the most budget-conscious shopper can't remember the exact price of every product across multiple stores or weeks. Was milk $3.49 last time or $3.79? Was that detergent cheaper online or in-store? Retailers exploit this gap in memory, counting on you to absorb slow price creep without noticing.

How AI Spots Overpricing

AI tools are built for this kind of pattern recognition. By scanning receipts, loyalty accounts, or online carts, they can:

- **Compare across stores:** Flagging when your usual brand of pasta is $1.29 at Store A but $1.79 at Store B.
- **Track shrinkflation:** Alerting you when package sizes drop while prices stay the same.
- **Identify recurring markups:** Highlighting items that always carry a premium in certain stores or times of day.
- **Spot coupon mismatches:** Pointing out when a sale price isn't actually the lowest available deal.

Instead of guessing, you see hard data on where your money is leaking.

Real-World Example

One AI shopping assistant flagged that a customer's grocery delivery service was adding a "service markup" of 10–15% to item prices— on top of delivery and tip. Over six months, that translated to **$312 in unnecessary charges.** Without AI crunching the numbers, the customer would never have noticed.

Action, Not Just Awareness

Awareness is only half the solution. Many AI apps now suggest direct fixes:

- Recommending cheaper store alternatives.
- Applying digital coupons automatically.
- Building shopping lists optimized for price and quality.

Some even allow you to set price alerts: *"Notify me when chicken breast drops below $2.50/lb."*

Takeaway: Grocery and retail overpricing thrives in the shadows of forgetfulness and complexity. AI brings clarity, scanning patterns, flagging markups, and turning invisible waste into visible savings. With automation doing the math, you no longer have to wonder if you're overpaying—you'll know, and you'll have the tools to stop it.

Dynamic Pricing Online (AI vs. Algorithms)

When you shop online, you probably assume the price you see is the same price everyone else sees. It's not. Behind the scenes, retailers use *dynamic pricing*—an algorithm that adjusts prices in real time based on demand, competition, and even your personal browsing habits. Two customers could look at the exact same product but see two very different prices.

How Retailers Use Dynamic Pricing Against You

Dynamic pricing was pioneered by airlines and hotels but has now spread to nearly every corner of e-commerce. Retailers analyze your data—location, purchase history, browsing patterns, even the type of device you're using—and tweak prices accordingly.

Examples include:

- **Returning visitor penalties:** If you check the same product multiple times, the price may rise, pressuring you to "buy before it goes higher."
- **Location-based adjustments:** Shoppers in wealthier ZIP codes may see higher prices than those in other areas.
- **Device targeting:** Some platforms have historically shown higher prices to iPhone users than Android users, assuming a higher willingness to pay.

The result? You might pay $20 more for the same item than the person next door.

Why You Rarely Notice

Dynamic pricing works because it's invisible. Unless you're comparing across multiple accounts and devices, you'll never know if you got the "best price." And because prices change constantly, you can't rely on memory to spot increases.

How AI Levels the Playing Field

AI can fight back by detecting and exploiting the same patterns retailers use. Here's how:

- **Price history tracking:** AI shopping assistants can show you a product's pricing over weeks or months, exposing sudden spikes that aren't "special deals" but manufactured urgency.
- **Cross-platform comparison:** Instead of checking five different sites, AI compares them instantly, showing you the true lowest price available.
- **Anonymous browsing:** Some AI-powered tools mask your identity or location, preventing retailers from targeting you with inflated prices.
- **Automated alerts:** AI can notify you when the price of an item drops below your target level, ensuring you buy at the right moment—not when retailers want you to.

Real-World Example

One customer used an AI shopping extension to track the price of a new laptop. The retailer's site showed $1,199—but the AI revealed that the same model had been $999 two weeks earlier and flagged a competitor selling it for $1,029. Armed with this data, the customer avoided paying nearly $200 more than necessary.

The Battle of Algorithms

Dynamic pricing is essentially *retail algorithms vs. you.* Without AI, you're playing a rigged game. With AI, you fight fire with fire—using algorithms to expose manipulation and secure fairer prices.

Takeaway: Online prices aren't fixed—they're fluid, shaped by algorithms designed to maximize profit. AI gives you the power to see through the manipulation, track true value, and buy on your terms. In the battle of algorithms, you don't have to be outmatched—you just need smarter tools.

Using Cashback, Rewards, and Smart Coupons Automatically

Everyone loves the idea of saving money with coupons, cashback offers, or reward points. But in practice, most people miss out. Coupons expire, cashback sites require extra clicks, and reward points often go unused. The problem isn't lack of opportunity—it's the friction involved. That's exactly what AI eliminates: it automates savings so you never have to think about them.

Why We Miss Easy Savings

- **Coupons:** Most people forget to search before checkout—or waste time on expired codes that don't work.
- **Cashback programs:** They often require remembering to go through a specific portal before making a purchase.
- **Reward points:** Credit card or retailer rewards sit unused because tracking them takes effort.

Billions of dollars in unclaimed savings and points expire each year simply because people forget or give up.

How AI Automates the Process

AI-powered shopping assistants sit quietly in your browser or phone, activating savings in real time:

- **Coupon automation:** The AI tests every available coupon at checkout and applies the best one automatically. No more copy-pasting expired codes.
- **Cashback activation:** Instead of remembering to visit a cashback portal, AI triggers the rebate automatically whenever you shop at a participating site.
- **Reward optimization:** Some AI tools connect to your credit cards and loyalty programs, then recommend which card or account gives the highest rewards for each purchase.

In short, you don't have to change behavior—AI simply layers extra savings on top of what you're already buying.

Real-World Example

A customer shopping online for clothes had a cart totaling $142. The AI assistant automatically applied a 15% coupon, activated 5% cashback, and suggested switching from a debit card to a credit card that offered triple reward points for retail purchases. The total value of these automatic optimizations: **$38 saved on a single order.**

Why This Matters

Manually stacking coupons, cashback, and rewards is like juggling—it works if you're meticulous, but most people drop the ball. AI removes the juggling act. It turns potential savings into guaranteed savings, ensuring you never leave money on the table.

Compounding Over Time

Saving $10 or $20 here and there may not feel life-changing—but repeated across a year, automated cashback and coupon use can easily add up to **$300–$600 per household.** Combine that with optimized reward redemptions, and you're reclaiming money that would have quietly expired.

Takeaway: Cashback, rewards, and coupons are only valuable if you actually use them. AI ensures you do—automatically, without effort, and without the frustration of expired codes or forgotten points. What once felt like a chore becomes a background system that saves you money every time you shop.

Mini-Guide: How to Set Up a "Smart Shopper" AI Agent

You don't need to become a tech expert to unlock the power of AI in your daily shopping. Setting up a "smart shopper" AI agent takes less than an hour—and once it's running, it works in the background every time you shop. Here's a simple step-by-step guide.

Step 1: Choose Your AI Shopping Assistant

There are multiple AI-powered tools designed to save you money while shopping online. Look for features like:

- Automatic coupon application at checkout.
- Cashback activation.
- Price tracking and alerts.
- Rewards card optimization.

Some tools work as browser extensions (like Chrome or Safari add-ons), while others are mobile apps that monitor your purchases.

Step 2: Connect Your Accounts Securely

Link your email, loyalty cards, and (if you're comfortable) your credit cards. This allows the AI to:

- Track receipts for hidden markups.
- Monitor expiring rewards points.
- Suggest the best payment method for each purchase.

Most tools use bank-grade encryption for security. Always confirm that the platform is reputable and transparent about data use.

Step 3: Set Price Alerts for Key Items

If you regularly buy the same products—like groceries, household items, or electronics—set AI alerts. Example:

- "Notify me when ground beef drops below $3/lb."
- "Alert me if this laptop falls under $1,000."

Instead of chasing sales, you let AI bring them to you.

Step 4: Automate Cashback and Coupons

Enable automatic cashback so you never need to click through a separate portal. Then, turn on coupon auto-testing. The AI will try every available code at checkout and apply the best one instantly.

This step alone can save **hundreds annually** with zero effort.

Step 5: Optimize Your Rewards

If you use multiple credit cards, AI can recommend the best one for each transaction. For example, it might say:

- "Use your travel rewards card for this flight to earn 3x miles."
- "Use your retail card for this purchase to get 5% cashback."

It ensures you maximize rewards without memorizing complex rules.

Step 6: Review Your Savings Monthly

Most AI shopping tools include a dashboard that shows how much you've saved. Take five minutes once a month to review. Seeing the numbers grow isn't just motivating—it reinforces that your system is working.

The Smart Shopper Mindset

The goal isn't to chase every deal or obsess over prices—it's to set up systems that quietly protect your wallet. Once your AI agent is in place, you can shop the way you always do, knowing the savings happen automatically.

Takeaway: A "smart shopper" AI agent is like having a personal assistant who never forgets a coupon, never misses a cashback opportunity, and never lets rewards points expire. With one quick setup, you create a lifelong habit of saving money every time you shop—without changing your behavior.

CHAPTER 7

Scam Proofing Your Wallet

Why Scams Are Exploding (Especially for Seniors)

Scams are not new—but they've never been more profitable. In 2023 alone, Americans lost over **$10 billion to fraud**, the highest number ever recorded. And the trend is accelerating. Scammers are getting smarter, technology is making them harder to detect, and economic stress makes people more vulnerable to promises of quick fixes. But one group is especially targeted: seniors.

Why Scams Are Growing Overall

Several factors explain the surge:

1. **Digital Everywhere**
   Banking, shopping, and communication have all moved online. Every digital touchpoint—email, text, social media, even phone apps—becomes a potential entry point for fraud.
2. **Low Cost, High Reward**
   Running a scam doesn't require much money. A laptop, an internet connection, and stolen email lists can reach millions of people instantly. Even if only 1 in 10,000 victims falls for it, scammers profit.
3. **AI-Powered Deception**
   Ironically, the same AI tools that help consumers save money are being exploited by criminals. Scammers use AI to create realistic phishing emails, fake websites, and even cloned voices that sound like a friend or relative asking for help.
4. **Economic Anxiety**
   Periods of inflation and financial stress make people more receptive to "too good to be true" offers—like quick loan approvals, government refunds, or investment opportunities. Scammers prey on fear and hope in equal measure.

Why Seniors Are Prime Targets

While anyone can fall victim, seniors are disproportionately affected. In 2022, older adults reported nearly **$1.7 billion in losses** to fraud, and experts believe the true number is much higher because many cases go unreported.

Here's why:

- **Less Familiarity with Tech:** Many seniors didn't grow up in the digital world, making it harder to spot fake websites, suspicious links, or scam apps.
- **Trust in Authority:** Seniors are more likely to answer phone calls, read mail carefully, and assume legitimacy when someone claims to be from the bank, IRS, or Social Security.
- **Isolation:** Scammers exploit loneliness by building fake relationships through romance scams or "grandparent scams," where a fraudster pretends to be a grandchild in trouble.
- **Financial Vulnerability:** Seniors often control retirement savings or fixed incomes, making them attractive targets for anyone looking for large, quick payouts.

The Human Cost

For seniors, scam losses aren't just financial—they're emotional. Victims often feel ashamed or embarrassed, which prevents them from seeking help. This silence allows scammers to keep operating unchecked. Worse, many victims don't just lose money once— they're placed on "sucker lists" that circulate among criminals, leading to repeated targeting.

Why This Matters to Everyone

You don't have to be a senior to be at risk. The same tactics—phishing emails, fake customer support calls, fraudulent subscriptions—are aimed at younger consumers too. But understanding why scams hit older adults hardest helps us all see the larger pattern: criminals thrive where technology outpaces awareness.

Takeaway: Scams are exploding because digital technology makes fraud cheaper, faster, and harder to detect. Seniors face the greatest risk due to trust, isolation, and unfamiliarity with online systems—but no one is immune. Recognizing the scope of the problem is the first step toward building defenses, especially with AI tools designed to spot scams before they strike.

AI as Your 24/7 Fraud Detector

Scammers never sleep. They send phishing emails at midnight, spoof calls during lunch breaks, and push fake charges onto accounts at random hours. No human can monitor every inbox, text message, and bank statement around the clock. But AI can. By acting as a 24/7 fraud detector, AI tools give you the kind of constant vigilance that used to be impossible.

How Fraud Slips Through

Traditional protections—like reviewing monthly statements or relying on spam filters—are reactive. By the time you notice, the money is gone. Worse, scammers are evolving faster than banks can update their defenses. Fake emails now look professional, fraudulent websites mimic real ones, and scam charges hide under vague descriptions like "SERVICE FEE" or "ONLINE PAYMENT."

The result? Even cautious consumers can get fooled.

What AI Does Differently

AI fraud detectors are trained to spot patterns no human could catch. Instead of just looking for obvious red flags (like misspelled words in an email), they analyze:

- **Transaction patterns:** Flagging purchases outside your usual habits (e.g., a charge in another country).
- **Login behavior:** Alerting you if someone signs into your account from an unusual device.
- **Communication cues:** Scanning emails or texts for subtle phishing markers, even when the message looks legitimate.
- **Subscription anomalies:** Detecting recurring charges that don't match your purchase history.

AI doesn't just rely on blacklists of known scams—it learns continuously, adapting as scammers invent new tricks.

Real-Time Intervention

The biggest advantage of AI is speed. Instead of finding out weeks later, you're alerted immediately:

- *"Unusual login detected from Brazil. Is this you?"*
- *"$249 charge pending from unfamiliar vendor. Approve or block?"*
- *"This email claiming to be from your bank is flagged as suspicious."*

In many cases, AI can automatically freeze suspicious transactions until you confirm, preventing losses before they happen.

The Human + AI Partnership

AI isn't perfect. Some alerts will be false alarms, and no system catches 100% of scams. But the combination of human judgment and AI speed is powerful. AI filters the noise, surfacing only what matters. You stay in control, but with far less effort.

Think of it as having a financial bodyguard: you don't need to be paranoid or hypervigilant—your AI assistant watches your back around the clock.

Takeaway: Scammers rely on timing, surprise, and the limits of human attention. AI flips the advantage by monitoring 24/7, catching fraud in real time, and blocking threats before they cost you money. With an AI fraud detector in place, you're no longer an easy target—you're protected by a system that never blinks.

Recognizing Fake Subscriptions and Fraudulent Vendors

Not all scams come as obvious "Nigerian prince" emails or suspicious phone calls. Increasingly, fraud hides in plain sight—disguised as subscriptions or online vendors that look completely legitimate. These schemes exploit the rise of auto-pay culture and digital marketplaces, where small recurring charges or one-time payments slip by unnoticed.

The Rise of Fake Subscriptions

Fraudsters know that most people don't track every $4.99 or $9.99 charge. That's why fake subscription scams are exploding. Here's how they work:

1. You sign up for a free trial of an app, service, or website.
2. The fine print enrolls you in an auto-renewing subscription.
3. Canceling is deliberately difficult—or impossible.

Some of these services deliver nothing at all. Others provide low-value "reports" or "digital toolkits" designed to look legitimate while draining your account every month.

Worse, scammers often use vague billing descriptors—like *"ONLINE SERVICES 123"*—to make charges blend in with your legitimate transactions.

Fraudulent Vendors and Fake Stores

E-commerce scams are another growing threat. Criminals set up convincing websites or marketplace profiles offering popular products at discounted prices. Once you pay, you either receive a counterfeit product, a low-quality substitute, or nothing at all.

Red flags include:

- Prices far below market value.
- No clear return/refund policy.
- Poorly written customer service responses.
- Payment required only via gift card, wire transfer, or cryptocurrency.

Because these vendors often disappear after a few weeks, pursuing refunds becomes nearly impossible.

Why People Fall for These Scams

- **Trust in automation:** Once a subscription is on auto-pay, most people stop thinking about it.
- **Professional design:** Fake vendors often mimic the look of real companies with logos, checkout systems, and "secure" seals.
- **The small-charge strategy:** Charges under $10 rarely trigger alarms, but multiplied across thousands of victims, they generate millions in profit.

How AI Spots the Fakes

AI tools are uniquely equipped to detect these scams:

- **Subscription monitoring:** AI can scan for duplicate or suspicious recurring payments and flag services you've never used.
- **Vendor analysis:** AI cross-references seller reputations, customer reviews, and shipping patterns to warn you before you buy.
- **Language scanning:** Fraudulent sites often share common markers—generic product descriptions, recycled stock images—that AI can spot instantly.
- **Behavioral alerts:** If you suddenly sign up for multiple new subscriptions, AI may flag it as unusual behavior worth double-checking.

Example in Action

One user connected their bank account to an AI financial assistant, which quickly flagged a $7.99 monthly subscription labeled *"TechProtect Services."* The user had never heard of the company. After investigation, it turned out to be a fraudulent service exploiting leaked credit card data. Without AI's alert, those charges could have continued indefinitely.

Takeaway: Fake subscriptions and fraudulent vendors thrive on invisibility—small charges, convincing websites, and vague billing that slip under the radar. AI makes them visible by scanning patterns, analyzing vendors, and warning you before money leaves your account. With the right tools, you don't just spot scams after the fact—you prevent them before they drain your wallet.

Checklist: Family Safety Plan Against Fraud

Scams aren't just an individual problem—they affect entire families. A parent might fall for a fake subscription, a grandparent might answer a phishing call, or a teenager might download a scam app. The best defense is a coordinated plan that protects everyone. Think of it like installing locks on your financial house. Here's a simple, practical checklist you can put in place today.

---

1. Centralize Account Monitoring

- Connect all family bank accounts, credit cards, and digital wallets to a trusted AI financial assistant.
- Ensure every household member knows that the AI will send alerts if unusual charges appear.

Why it matters: Scams thrive on hidden activity. A central watchdog keeps every account under surveillance.

---

2. Share the "Red Flag" List

Teach everyone to recognize common scam markers:

- Urgent requests ("Act now or lose access!").
- Unusual payment methods (gift cards, wire transfers, crypto only).
- Vague company names on bank statements.
- Unsolicited calls or emails claiming to be from banks or government agencies.

Why it matters: Awareness is the first line of defense—especially for seniors and teens.

---

3. Use Strong, Unique Passwords

- Enable a password manager for the whole family.
- Turn on two-factor authentication (2FA) for all financial accounts.

Why it matters: Weak or reused passwords are one of the easiest entry points for scammers.

---

4. Set Up AI Alerts for Everyone

- Configure AI tools to send text/email alerts for suspicious logins, bill hikes, or unusual purchases.
- Encourage family members to *never ignore* alerts—even if they seem minor.

Why it matters: Real-time alerts stop fraud before it snowballs.

---

5. Establish a Family "Pause Rule"

Agree that no one will send money, share account details, or sign up for a subscription without pausing to double-check with another family member.

Why it matters: Scammers prey on urgency. A quick pause breaks their momentum.

6. Run an Annual "Scam Drill"

Once a year, sit down as a family and:

- Review recent scam trends (AI can generate reports).
- Check that all accounts are secured with strong passwords.
- Update your AI monitoring tools.

Why it matters: Just like fire drills, practicing scam awareness builds habits that stick.

Building a Family Firewall

Fraud prevention isn't about paranoia—it's about preparation. When everyone in the family follows the same safety plan, scammers lose their biggest advantage: surprise. Instead of reacting after money disappears, you prevent fraud before it happens.

Takeaway: Scams target the most vulnerable link in the family chain. A shared safety plan—powered by AI monitoring, simple rules, and open communication—turns your family into a united defense system. With everyone on the same page, fraud attempts are spotted early, and money stays where it belongs: with you.

CHAPTER 8

Budgeting Without Spreadsheets: Let AI Do the Math

Traditional Budgeting vs. AI-Assisted Forecasting

For decades, the gold standard of personal finance has been the humble budget. Whether on paper, in a spreadsheet, or inside an app, the idea was the same: track what you earn, track what you spend, and make sure the numbers balance. But in today's world of subscriptions, dynamic pricing, hidden fees, and fluctuating bills, traditional budgeting simply can't keep up. That's why AI-assisted forecasting is fast becoming the smarter, easier alternative.

Why Traditional Budgeting Breaks Down

1. **It's Backward-Looking**
   Budgets show where your money *went*—not where it's going. You only see problems after they've happened, like discovering you overspent weeks later when the damage is already done.
2. **It's Time-Consuming**
   Manual tracking requires entering transactions, categorizing expenses, and constantly updating spreadsheets. Even with apps, most systems still rely on you to do the heavy lifting.
3. **It Assumes Predictability**
   Life doesn't fit neatly into budget categories. A flat tire, a birthday dinner, or an unexpected medical bill blows the numbers out of balance. Most people give up when their "perfect plan" doesn't survive real life.
4. **It Relies on Willpower**
   Budgets assume you'll act like a robot—never forgetting to log expenses, always sticking to limits. The moment you slip, guilt sets in, and many abandon the system entirely.

How AI-Assisted Forecasting Changes the Game

Instead of looking backward, AI looks forward. By analyzing your income, spending patterns, bills, and even seasonal habits, AI can predict what your finances will look like weeks or months ahead.

Here's what that means in practice:

- **Bill Prediction:** AI knows your utility bill rises in winter and forecasts the increase before it hits.
- **Spending Trends:** It sees that you typically overspend on dining out toward the end of each month and warns you early.
- **Cash Flow Alerts:** It forecasts when your balance will dip too low, preventing overdraft fees before they happen.
- **Scenario Testing:** It shows how a vacation, new subscription, or debt payment will impact your finances over time.

Instead of reactive tracking, you get proactive guidance.

Example in Action

Imagine you're planning a holiday trip. A spreadsheet would only show how much you've spent *after* the trip is over. AI-assisted forecasting, on the other hand, can run scenarios:

- If you book flights now, you'll have $1,200 left in checking by month's end.
- If you wait until payday, you'll avoid dipping below your savings threshold.
- If you reduce dining-out by $100 this month, you can cover trip costs without touching your emergency fund.

That's not budgeting—it's financial navigation.

Why It Feels Different

The biggest shift is psychological. Traditional budgets feel like restrictions: "Don't overspend here, don't go over there." AI forecasting feels like support: "Here's how to get what you want without hurting your future." One system nags, the other guides.

Takeaway: Traditional budgeting is a rear-view mirror—useful for reflection but powerless to prevent mistakes. AI-assisted forecasting is a GPS for your money: it shows you where you're headed, alerts you to risks, and helps you reroute in real time. The result is less stress, fewer surprises, and a plan that actually fits real life.

How AI Builds Realistic Budgets from Your Data

Traditional budgets often collapse under the weight of unrealistic expectations. They assume you'll spend exactly $300 on groceries, exactly $150 on dining, and exactly $80 on transportation every month. Real life doesn't work that way. Spending fluctuates. Bills creep. Emergencies happen. That's why so many people abandon budgets after a few months—they're too rigid to match reality. AI budgeting flips the model: instead of forcing you into a template, it learns from your actual financial behavior and adapts around it.

From Categories to Context

Instead of generic categories, AI looks at how *you* actually spend. It doesn't assume everyone should budget the same way. For example:

- If you consistently spend more on groceries but little on entertainment, AI will re-balance your budget automatically instead of labeling you as "over."
- If your utilities spike every winter, AI builds seasonal variation into your plan.

- If you earn income from gig work, AI accounts for fluctuations instead of assuming a fixed paycheck.

The result is a budget that reflects reality—not one that punishes you for being human.

The Power of Pattern Recognition

AI thrives on data patterns. By analyzing months (or even years) of transactions, it can detect:

- **Recurring expenses:** Subscriptions, memberships, regular bills.
- **Irregular but predictable costs:** Annual insurance, holiday shopping, tax payments.
- **Behavioral rhythms:** You may spend more on weekends or at the end of the month.

Once these patterns are identified, AI forecasts them into the future—so you're prepared before the charges hit.

Continuous Adjustment

Unlike static spreadsheets, AI budgets evolve. Every time you spend or earn, the system recalibrates. If you go over in one category, AI shifts resources from another. If you save on groceries one week, AI shows how that buffer improves your monthly outlook.

It's budgeting as a *living system*, not a rigid plan.

Example in Action

Take Alex, who used to abandon budgeting apps after two months of "failing." His AI-driven budget, however, recognized that he always overspent on dining by $50 but underspent on transportation. Instead of scolding him, the AI adjusted the categories—keeping his overall balance intact while reflecting his real habits. For the first time, Alex stuck with a budget for the full year—because it finally felt doable.

Why This Matters

Most people don't need more discipline—they need better systems. AI delivers a budget that adapts as fast as life does. Instead of guilt and frustration, you get clarity and confidence.

Takeaway: AI builds budgets from the ground up, based on your actual data and habits. By recognizing patterns, adapting dynamically, and forecasting ahead, it creates a plan that works *with you* instead of against you. The result is a realistic, flexible system you can actually stick to—without spreadsheets or shame.

Automating Savings Goals (Vacation, Debt, Emergency Fund)

Most people know they *should* save—for a vacation, to pay off debt faster, or to build an emergency fund. The problem isn't knowledge. The problem is consistency. After bills and daily expenses, saving often gets whatever scraps are left. That's why financial experts say, *"Pay yourself first."* But willpower isn't enough. Life gets in the way. This is where AI transforms saving: by automating it intelligently, based on your actual cash flow.

The Old Way: Saving on Leftovers

Traditional advice tells you to set aside a fixed percentage each month, like 10% of your paycheck. But that only works if your income and expenses are perfectly stable. If one month brings car repairs or higher utility bills, you either skip saving or dip into what you set aside. Over time, this inconsistency erodes progress.

The AI Way: Dynamic Saving

AI-powered budgeting tools don't treat saving as an afterthought—
they build it into your financial plan dynamically. Here's how:

1. **Analyzing cash flow:** AI learns when you typically have
   extra funds (like right after payday).
2. **Predicting upcoming expenses:** It knows when rent,
   utilities, or subscriptions will hit.
3. **Calculating safe transfers:** Based on your habits, it
   automatically moves money into savings without risking
   overdraft.

Instead of you deciding how much to save, AI continuously adjusts,
ensuring steady progress even when life fluctuates.

Vacation Savings

Want to take a $2,000 trip in eight months? AI breaks it down:
$250/month or about $8/day. It then creates micro-savings—
rounding up purchases or pulling small amounts on low-spend
days—so you reach the goal without feeling the pinch.

Debt Paydown

Paying off debt faster is one of the most powerful uses of AI
automation. Instead of sticking to minimum payments, AI can
allocate extra cash toward your highest-interest balances, shaving
months (or years) off repayment. It's like having a financial coach
redirect spare dollars where they'll have the biggest impact.

Emergency Fund

Experts recommend 3–6 months of living expenses in an emergency fund, but that feels overwhelming for most people. AI reframes it as a series of manageable steps: start with $500, then $1,000, then keep building. Each time your cash flow allows, AI nudges extra funds into the account—no big sacrifices required.

Example in Action

Jamie wanted to save $1,200 for holiday gifts while paying off a credit card balance. AI split her surplus funds automatically: 70% toward debt, 30% toward holiday savings. By the end of six months, she'd cut her credit card interest charges by $180 *and* paid cash for gifts—without once sitting down to do the math herself.

Takeaway: Saving doesn't have to depend on discipline or leftovers. AI automates the process—breaking goals into bite-sized chunks, adjusting dynamically to your cash flow, and making steady progress in the background. Whether it's a dream vacation, faster debt payoff, or financial safety net, AI ensures your goals don't just stay goals— they actually happen.

Worksheet: 30-Day AI-Assisted Budget Plan

You don't need months of preparation or complicated spreadsheets to experience how AI can transform your money management. In fact, you can start today and see results within 30 days. Use this simple worksheet as your starter plan. Think of it as a guided experiment: you'll set up AI, let it run in the background, and check in once a week.

Step 1: Connect Your Accounts (Day 1–2)

- Link your checking, savings, and credit card accounts to a trusted AI budgeting tool.
- Enable transaction monitoring so the AI can see your real cash flow.

✅ *Goal:* Create a single dashboard that shows all your money in one place.

Step 2: Establish Baselines (Day 3–7)

- Let the AI categorize your expenses automatically (groceries, bills, subscriptions, etc.).
- Review its first report: Which categories are higher than you expected? Which are lower?

✅ *Goal:* Identify your biggest leaks without manually tracking anything.

Step 3: Set One Savings Goal (Day 8–10)

- Choose one short-term goal: vacation fund, $200 toward debt, or building a $300 emergency cushion.
- Tell the AI your goal and deadline.

✅ *Goal:* Have the AI break your target into manageable weekly or daily savings steps.

Step 4: Turn On Smart Alerts (Day 11–15)

- Enable notifications for:
  - Bill hikes
  - Duplicate/unused subscriptions
  - Upcoming large expenses
- Approve at least one action the AI recommends (e.g., canceling a subscription).

✅ *Goal:* Catch at least one money leak before it drains you.

Step 5: Automate Micro-Savings (Day 16–20)

- Activate AI round-ups (e.g., spend $3.25 → $0.75 goes into savings).
- Let AI move small amounts ($5–$10) into savings when your balance is strong.

✅ *Goal:* Watch your savings grow without feeling a squeeze.

Step 6: Run a Forecast (Day 21–25)

- Use the AI's forecasting tool to see where your balance will be in 30, 60, or 90 days.
- Adjust one spending habit based on its prediction (e.g., reduce takeout by $40 to avoid overdraft).

✅ *Goal:* Prevent at least one future problem before it happens.

Step 7: Review and Reset (Day 26–30)

- Open your AI dashboard and review: How much did you save? What leaks did you plug?
- Decide on one new goal for the next 30 days (e.g., increase savings target, add a debt repayment plan).

☑ *Goal:* End the month with more money in your pocket—and momentum for the next round.

Why This Works

This 30-day plan works because it's realistic. You're not being asked to overhaul your entire financial life or track every dollar manually. Instead, you're letting AI do the hard work—tracking, analyzing, forecasting, and nudging—while you make small, high-impact decisions.

By the end of one month, most people save **$100–$300** they would have otherwise lost to leaks, forgotten subscriptions, or inefficient spending. That's not theory—that's proof that AI-driven budgeting can deliver results fast.

Takeaway: Budgeting doesn't have to be a grind. With this 30-day AI-assisted plan, you'll experience firsthand how automation removes the stress, spots the leaks, and builds momentum toward your goals. Once you see the difference, you'll never go back to spreadsheets.

CHAPTER 9

Building Your Personal Money Autopilot

How to Safely Connect Accounts and Data

The idea of connecting your financial accounts to an AI system can feel intimidating. After all, we've all heard horror stories of hacks, leaks, and stolen information. But the truth is, AI-powered money tools don't work without access to your data. They need to see your spending, bills, and subscriptions to help you cut waste and build your autopilot system. The good news? With the right precautions, you can connect your accounts safely and confidently—often with stronger protections than you already use for online banking.

Why Connection Is Necessary

To build a "money autopilot," the AI needs to:

- **Track transactions:** Spot recurring charges, fees, and bill hikes.
- **Forecast cash flow:** Predict dips and surpluses in your account.
- **Automate savings and payments:** Move money into savings goals or pay off debt automatically.

Without this connection, you're only getting half the benefit—the AI is essentially blind.

How Data Security Works

Reputable financial AI platforms use the same encryption standards as banks (often called **256-bit encryption**). That means even if the data were intercepted, it would be unreadable. On top of that, most services don't store your login credentials directly. Instead, they use **secure tokens** issued by your bank. These tokens allow "read-only" access—meaning the AI can see your transactions but cannot move money without your explicit permission.

Think of it like giving a telescope to someone outside your house: they can see what's happening, but they can't open the door or touch anything inside.

Safety Best Practices

To connect accounts safely, follow these steps:

1. **Choose trusted providers.** Look for AI tools that partner with established financial data companies like Plaid or Yodlee, which are widely used by banks and payment apps.
2. **Enable multi-factor authentication (MFA).** Always turn on 2FA or MFA for your bank accounts and the AI tool itself. This ensures that even if your password is compromised, access is blocked without a second confirmation step.
3. **Limit permissions.** Start with read-only connections. Only allow transfer capabilities if you're comfortable with automation—and even then, enable alerts so you're notified of every action.
4. **Use unique passwords.** Never reuse banking passwords for financial apps. A password manager can create and store unique logins securely.
5. **Check compliance.** Reputable tools will clearly state they are compliant with financial privacy standards (such as GDPR or CCPA in the U.S.). If they don't mention this, walk away.

Peace of Mind Through Transparency

The best AI tools make their security policies transparent. They explain how your data is encrypted, who has access (often no one at the company itself), and what actions the system can and cannot take. If a tool feels secretive about these details, that's a red flag.

Example in Action

Consider Sarah, who was hesitant to link her accounts to an AI budgeting app. After confirming it used token-based access and had no ability to transfer money without her approval, she connected her checking and credit card accounts. Within 48 hours, the AI flagged two unused subscriptions costing her $23/month. That's $276 per year—found immediately—without compromising her safety.

Takeaway: Connecting your accounts to AI isn't a leap of blind trust—it's a strategic move, provided you follow best practices. With encryption, tokenized access, and clear permissions, you can safely unlock the full power of financial automation while keeping control of your money and your data.

Creating Your Autopilot Dashboard

Once your accounts are safely connected, the next step is building your **autopilot dashboard**—a single control center where you can see, at a glance, what's happening with your money. Instead of juggling multiple apps, bank portals, and spreadsheets, the dashboard consolidates everything into one place. It's not just a convenience feature—it's the brain of your financial autopilot.

Why a Dashboard Matters

Most financial stress doesn't come from the actual numbers—it comes from the *uncertainty*. Am I overspending? Did that bill get paid? Do I have enough for next month? The dashboard eliminates guesswork by providing real-time visibility. In one screen, you know:

- How much cash you have available.
- Which bills are upcoming.
- How much is going toward savings or debt.
- Whether there are any unusual charges.

Think of it as your financial cockpit: one glance tells you if everything is on course—or if you need to make adjustments.

What Your Dashboard Should Include

A strong autopilot dashboard has four key elements:

1. **Cash Flow Overview**
   - Income received, bills paid, and your current balance.
   - Projected balances for the next 30–60 days, based on AI forecasts.
2. **Subscriptions & Recurring Charges**
   - A list of all ongoing subscriptions.
   - Notifications about free trials ending or price hikes.
3. **Savings & Goals Tracker**
   - Progress toward specific goals (vacation, debt payoff, emergency fund).
   - Automated updates when micro-savings or round-ups are added.
4. **Alerts & Action Items**
   - Suspicious transactions flagged for review.
   - Bills flagged as negotiable or overpriced.
   - Reminders for tasks like insurance reviews or renewals.

Customizing Your Dashboard

Not all dashboards are created equal. Some are packed with charts and data, which can feel overwhelming. The goal is clarity, not clutter. Customization is key:

- If you care most about debt payoff, make that front and center.
- If you want peace of mind, highlight cash flow projections.
- If you're saving for multiple goals, track progress visually with progress bars.

Your dashboard should motivate action, not bury you in numbers.

Example in Action

David, a teacher with a busy schedule, set up his autopilot dashboard in less than an hour. He customized it to show:

- His monthly paycheck deposits.
- Upcoming bills for utilities and rent.
- His emergency fund growth.
- Any unusual charges.

Within the first week, the dashboard flagged a $14.99 subscription he didn't recognize. He canceled it in one click. That small win built trust in the system—and freed up money to redirect toward his emergency fund.

The Power of One Screen

The genius of the autopilot dashboard isn't that it shows you *everything*—it's that it shows you what matters most, when you need to see it. Instead of worrying about what's happening with your money, you can check in once a week, make quick decisions, and let AI handle the rest.

Takeaway: Your autopilot dashboard is the heart of your financial system. It replaces uncertainty with clarity, guesswork with foresight, and stress with confidence. With all your accounts, goals, and alerts in one place, you finally gain control—not by doing more work, but by seeing clearly.

Automating Cancellations, Renegotiations, Reminders

You don't build a money autopilot by staring at dashboards—you build it by wiring *actions* to happen without you. Cancellations, renegotiations, and reminders are the three levers that recapture money every month with almost no ongoing effort. This section shows you how to turn each lever on, safely.

Why Automation Beats Good Intentions

Most leaks persist because they require friction: finding the login, locating the "cancel" link, sitting on hold, or remembering to renegotiate before a promo expires. Automation removes the parts your brain resists. Instead of "I should…," your system *does*—on schedule, with receipts.

Design principle: Automate anything that (1) repeats, (2) is time-sensitive, or (3) pays a predictable dividend when done.

What to Automate First (80/20)

1. **Cancellations:** Unused or duplicate subscriptions, free trials, legacy add-ons (e.g., device insurance you no longer need).
2. **Renegotiations:** Internet/phone (post-promo hikes), insurance renewals, software licenses, and annual memberships.
3. **Reminders:** Payment due dates, expiring trials, expiring promos, card statement closes, credit report checks, and annual "shop-around" dates.

Prioritize items with *recurring* savings. One automated cancellation that saves $14.99/month beats a one-time coupon every time.

Autopilot for Cancellations: From List to "Off"

Step 1: Detect. Link your accounts and inbox so your AI can surface active subscriptions, renewal dates, and last-use signals (e.g., no logins in 60–90 days).
Step 2: Rule it. Create rules like:

- *If* no use in 60 days **and** cost > $7/month → **queue cancel.**
- *If* duplicate category (two music apps) → **recommend keep one, cancel one.**
  Step 3: Execute. Where supported, enable "one-click cancel." For stubborn services, let the AI trigger a concierge workflow (prewritten email/chat script) and log the ticket number.
  Step 4: Verify. Require confirmation artifacts: cancellation email saved to a "Receipts/Cancellations" folder and a $0 future charge forecast.

Pro tip: Add a **grace tag**—"pause, don't cancel"—for seasonal services (e.g., language app). Your rule can auto-pause and set a 6-month reevaluation reminder.

Autopilot for Renegotiations: Set the Trap, Not the Alarm

Renegotiation is most effective when it's *timed* to price changes and renewal cycles.

Step 1: Triggers.

- Price hike detected (> $5 or > 8% vs. baseline).
- 30–60 days before contract end or insurance renewal date.
- Competitor price undercuts by > 10% for matching service.

Step 2: Script bank. Store AI-generated, provider-specific templates:

- *Retention script:* "Match competitor pricing or apply loyalty credit."
- *Bundle probe:* "What credits exist if I remove X and keep Y?"
- *Escalation:* "Please transfer to retention; I'm prepared to schedule cancellation."

Step 3: Channels. Preference order: chat (fast, documented) → secure message → phone (only if required). Your AI can launch chat, paste scripts, and capture transcript PDFs to your records.

Step 4: Decision rules.

- If offered ≥ 12-month rate lock or ≥ 15% cut → **accept**.
- If offered temporary promo < 3 months → **counter once**; if refused → **schedule provider switch** (AI can pre-fill the new order and pickup/return tasks).

Autopilot for Reminders: The Invisible Net

Reminders prevent late fees, overdrafts, and missed windows to save.

Set layered alerts:

- **7 days before**: Due date nudges for cards, utilities, rent.
- **2 days before**: "Pay minimum now" safety net (AI can schedule a minimum autopay to protect credit).
- **Statement close date**: "Make extra payment today to lower reported utilization."
- **Trials/promos**: 3-day and same-day cancel prompts; default to *auto-cancel unless you tap 'keep'*.

Add **once-a-year anchors**: insurance shop-around, credit report review, and a "subscription spring-clean."

Safety, Controls, and Audit Trail

Automation without control creates anxiety. Build guardrails:

- **Read-only first:** Start with detection and reminders. Enable money-moving only for specific workflows (e.g., minimum card autopay, savings transfers) with instant alerts.
- **Dollar caps:** "Never authorize a new recurring charge > $20 without confirmation."
- **Two-person rule (optional):** For family finances, require a second approval for plan changes over $200/year.
- **Receipts vault:** All actions (cancels, credits, new rates) stored automatically—email confirmations, chat transcripts, and revised bills—so disputes are one search away.

A 20-Minute Setup You'll Use for Years

1. **Link accounts + email** (read-only).
2. **Turn on detectors:** subscriptions, bill hikes, duplicate services.
3. **Create three rules:**
   - Unused > 60 days → queue cancel.
   - Hike > 8% → auto-launch renegotiation chat with script A.
   - Trials → auto-cancel at T-0 unless "keep."
4. **Enable minimum autopay** on all credit cards; add statement-close alerts.
5. **Schedule quarterly sweep:** AI compiles wins (savings total), pending actions, and upcoming renegotiations.

Real-World Illustration

Evan set these rules on a Sunday evening. By Friday:

- Two dormant apps auto-canceled: **$23.98/month saved.**
- Internet bill hike (+$12) triggered chat; AI secured a 12-month rollback and a $30 credit: **$174 saved this year.**
- Card statement-close alert nudged a $90 extra payment, dropping reported utilization and improving his score trajectory.
  Total week-one impact: **$462/year equivalent**—and zero hold music.

Takeaway: Dashboards inform; automations transform. When cancellations, renegotiations, and reminders run on rails—with clear rules and receipts—your finances start compounding small wins into permanent savings. That's money growth the effortless way: not by working harder, but by letting your systems do the work you would never consistently do yourself.

Step-by-Step: Your First 3 Automations to Set Up Today

Building a money autopilot doesn't mean you have to overhaul your entire financial system overnight. The fastest way to see results is to start small—set up just a few automations that deliver immediate savings and peace of mind. Here are three you can activate today.

1. Automate Subscription Detection & Cancellation

Why: Subscriptions are the most common source of money leaks. Even one forgotten $14.99/month app adds up to nearly $180 a year.

How to Set It Up:

1. Connect your bank and credit card accounts to an AI-powered financial tool.
2. Let it scan for recurring charges.
3. Review the list of active subscriptions it generates.
4. Cancel at least one unused or duplicate service directly through the app—or queue it with a one-click cancellation script.

Result: You stop paying for things you don't use, with savings that compound every single month.

---

2. Turn On Bill Hike Alerts

Why: Providers quietly raise prices by $5–$15 at a time, betting you won't notice. An AI alert ensures you catch every increase the moment it happens.

How to Set It Up:

1. Link your internet, phone, and utility bills to your AI dashboard.
2. Enable "bill monitoring" so the AI records your baseline price.
3. Turn on notifications for increases over a set threshold (e.g., $5 or 8%).
4. When you get an alert, use the AI's prewritten script to request a rollback or loyalty discount.

Result: You intercept price creep in real time and negotiate savings without spending hours on the phone.

3. Automate a Mini-Savings Transfer

Why: Most people wait to save "what's left over"—and end up saving nothing. Automating small transfers guarantees progress without requiring willpower.

How to Set It Up:

1. Pick one short-term goal (vacation fund, emergency cushion, debt payoff).
2. Tell your AI tool to automatically transfer a small amount— like $5/day or $50/week—into a separate savings account.
3. Enable "smart savings," which skips transfers if your balance is unusually low.

Result: You build momentum toward your goals without stress, and you'll see tangible progress within 30 days.

Why These 3 Work Together

- **Subscriptions** stop hidden leaks.
- **Bill alerts** prevent slow overcharging.
- **Automated savings** turn freed-up cash into forward progress.

Together, they form the foundation of your money autopilot: plug leaks, stop future losses, and grow savings automatically. Once these are in place, you can expand into bigger automations—like debt acceleration, insurance shopping, or investment contributions.

Takeaway: Don't wait for the "perfect" system. Set up just three automations today—subscription cancellations, bill hike alerts, and mini-savings transfers—and you'll feel the power of your money autopilot immediately. From there, every new automation compounds your control and your savings.

CHAPTER 10

Future-Proofing Your Finances with AI

What's Coming Next: AI in Taxes, Energy Bills, Travel Refunds

We've already seen how AI can cancel subscriptions, negotiate bills, and protect you from fraud. But that's just the beginning. The next wave of AI isn't about plugging leaks—it's about proactively creating savings in areas that most people don't even realize can be optimized: taxes, energy usage, and travel refunds. These aren't small wins. They're areas where the average household loses hundreds, sometimes thousands, of dollars a year simply because the systems are too complex to navigate alone.

AI in Taxes: Beyond Filing, Into Optimization

Tax season is stressful for one reason: complexity. The rules change every year, deductions are hidden in fine print, and most people leave money on the table. AI is poised to change this.

Instead of waiting until April to file, AI will monitor your finances year-round, suggesting tax-smart moves as you go:

- Flagging deductible expenses as soon as they hit your account.
- Advising whether to contribute to pre-tax retirement accounts to reduce taxable income.
- Identifying credits you're likely to qualify for based on your behavior (education, energy efficiency, healthcare).

Soon, AI will act like a real-time tax advisor, constantly running simulations in the background so you never miss a deduction or credit.

AI in Energy Bills: Smarter Homes, Smaller Costs

Utility companies have mastered the art of slow price creep. But AI is starting to fight back—by not just tracking bills, but actively reducing them.

- **Smart usage forecasting:** AI can analyze your past energy consumption and weather patterns to predict next month's bill. If a spike is coming, it alerts you early.
- **Appliance optimization:** Connected AI systems in smart homes can automatically adjust thermostats, water heaters, or appliances to minimize costs without sacrificing comfort.
- **Rate plan selection:** Many utility providers offer multiple rate plans, but they're confusing. AI can analyze your habits and recommend the plan that saves the most money.

In the future, your home won't just consume energy—it will constantly negotiate and optimize it for you.

AI in Travel Refunds: Never Lose to Fine Print Again

Anyone who's tried to get a travel refund knows how frustrating it is: hours on the phone, vague "terms and conditions," and credits you never use. AI can change that by monitoring your bookings in real time:

- **Price drop protection:** If your flight or hotel drops in price after you book, AI can request the refund automatically.
- **Delay and cancellation claims:** AI tools already exist that file compensation claims for delayed flights—sometimes securing hundreds of dollars you'd never have claimed yourself.
- **Refund reminders:** If you receive credits or vouchers, AI ensures they're tracked and used before they expire.

Instead of travel companies profiting from your inattention, AI ensures you always get the money you're entitled to.

The Bigger Picture

Taxes, energy, and travel refunds may seem unrelated, but they share one theme: **complexity that benefits companies, not consumers.** Governments, utilities, and travel providers all profit when you miss a deadline, overlook a clause, or fail to act. AI flips that dynamic by making complexity work *for* you instead of against you.

Takeaway: The next frontier of AI savings isn't just cutting waste— it's reclaiming money from the most complex financial systems we face: taxes, energy, and travel. These areas represent hundreds or even thousands of dollars in hidden opportunities each year. With AI running in the background, you'll stop losing to fine print and start winning by default.

Turning Small Annual Savings into Long-Term Wealth

It's easy to dismiss a $15 subscription cancellation or a $10 bill reduction as "no big deal." But here's the truth: the difference between people who stay stuck financially and those who build wealth often comes down to how they treat small wins. When managed intentionally—and especially when automated—those small annual savings compound into serious money.

The Psychology of "Just a Few Dollars"

Companies rely on you thinking: *"It's just a coffee," "It's just $9.99," "It's just a small fee."* Individually, these charges feel harmless. But the average household wastes over **$1,000 a year** on invisible leaks. The problem isn't that the amounts are small—it's that we ignore them. AI helps you collect those small wins systematically and funnel them into growth.

The Power of Compounding

Let's run the numbers:

- Saving $1,000 a year may not sound life-changing.
- But invest that $1,000 each year at a modest 7% annual return (historical stock market average).
- After 10 years: **$13,816.**
- After 20 years: **$43,865.**
- After 30 years: **$102,575.**

That's six figures, created entirely from money you would have otherwise wasted.

How AI Turns Savings into Growth

Here's where automation multiplies the impact:

- **Automatic transfers:** Every time AI cancels a subscription or secures a refund, it can transfer the money into savings or investments instead of letting it vanish into new spending.
- **Micro-investing:** Some tools automatically invest spare change from purchases into index funds or ETFs, turning pennies into long-term wealth.
- **Debt paydown first:** AI can prioritize directing savings into high-interest debt payoff, which can generate a guaranteed 15–25% "return" compared to leaving money idle.

This way, the moment you capture a savings win, it's put to work—growing quietly in the background.

Real-World Example

Chris used AI to save $87/month by canceling unused subscriptions and renegotiating his phone bill. Instead of letting that $87 disappear, he set up an auto-transfer into an investment account. After a year, he had over $1,000. After five years, with compounding, it grew to nearly $6,000. Chris didn't feel like he was "investing"—he just redirected money that was already wasted.

The Wealth Mindset Shift

The secret isn't earning more—it's keeping more, and putting it to work. AI makes this frictionless: find the leak, plug it, and automatically grow the difference. When repeated consistently, this builds wealth not through dramatic lifestyle changes, but through the quiet power of compounding.

Takeaway: Small annual savings are not small at all—they are seeds of long-term wealth. With AI capturing and redirecting them automatically, you don't just stop losing money—you start building a financial future where every dollar has a job, and every leak becomes growth.

Preparing for the "AI Everywhere" Decade

We are standing at the beginning of a financial revolution. In the next decade, AI won't just be a helpful add-on—it will be the default infrastructure of how money moves, how services are priced, and how consumers interact with companies. To thrive in this new landscape, you need to do more than adopt AI tools—you need to prepare for a world where AI is everywhere.

AI Won't Be Optional

Just as online banking went from novelty to necessity, AI-driven finance will follow the same path. Banks, insurers, retailers, and service providers are already embedding AI into their operations. That means the offers you see, the fees you're charged, and the negotiations you face will increasingly be handled by algorithms. If you're not using AI yourself, you'll be negotiating against machines with human limitations—attention, memory, and time.

From Reactive to Proactive Finance

The biggest mindset shift is this: you won't just use AI to react to problems, you'll rely on it to *anticipate* them. Instead of discovering a late fee, you'll be warned days in advance. Instead of scrambling to find the best insurance, your AI will automatically shop it for you. Instead of checking balances, your dashboard will tell you where you'll stand in 30, 60, or 90 days.

Financial success will no longer come from meticulous record-keeping—it will come from setting rules, letting automation run, and checking in briefly to approve or adjust.

New Threats, New Protections

Of course, scammers and corporations will use AI too. Expect:

- **Hyper-realistic fraud:** Deepfake voices, AI-written emails, and fake customer support sites that are nearly impossible to distinguish from the real thing.
- **Dynamic overpricing:** Companies using AI to charge you the maximum you're willing to pay.
- **Privacy risks:** More data collection, and more attempts to exploit it.

This makes your own AI protection non-negotiable. Fraud detectors, bill monitors, and price-comparison engines will be as essential as antivirus software once was.

Skills for the AI Decade

You don't need to become a programmer to benefit from AI. But you do need to:

1. **Get comfortable with automation.** Learn to trust systems that work in the background.
2. **Stay flexible.** New tools will keep emerging; be ready to test and adopt.
3. **Focus on oversight, not micromanagement.** Your role will shift from manual labor to strategic supervision.

Think of yourself less as a "budget keeper" and more as a *financial pilot*—setting direction, approving actions, and letting autopilot handle the turbulence.

The Long-Term Payoff

In the "AI everywhere" decade, the gap will widen between those who adopt AI and those who resist it. One group will quietly save thousands every year, build wealth automatically, and avoid scams. The other will fall further behind—overpaying, missing opportunities, and struggling to keep up.

The good news? You don't need to predict the future—you just need to set up systems now that adapt as AI evolves.

Takeaway: The future of money isn't manual. In the coming decade, AI will be embedded in every transaction, bill, and negotiation. Preparing today means embracing automation, strengthening fraud defenses, and shifting your role from financial micromanager to strategic overseer. With AI everywhere, the advantage belongs to those who let the machines do the work—while keeping human judgment in the driver's seat.

Action Plan: Your Roadmap for the Next 12 Months

Reading about AI tools is one thing. Using them to create real financial change is another. The key is to avoid overwhelm by starting small, then layering on new automations over time. Here's a month-by-month roadmap you can follow to future-proof your finances with AI in just one year.

Months 1–2: Build the Foundation

- **Connect your accounts:** Link checking, savings, and credit cards to a trusted AI budgeting tool.
- **Set up your dashboard:** Customize it to show cash flow, subscriptions, savings goals, and alerts.
- **Automate the basics:** Enable subscription detection, bill hike alerts, and a small automated savings transfer ($5–$10/day).

☑ *By the end of month 2, you'll already see at least $100–$300 in recovered savings.*

Months 3–4: Plug the Leaks

- **Cancel unused subscriptions:** Let the AI queue and execute cancellations.
- **Renegotiate bills:** Use AI scripts to roll back price hikes or lock in better rates.
- **Activate fraud alerts:** Turn on 24/7 monitoring for unusual charges, fake subscriptions, and phishing attempts.

☑ *By month 4, you should be saving $500+ per year on wasted fees and overcharges.*

Months 5–6: Optimize Insurance & Credit

- **Run an insurance comparison:** Have AI shop auto, home, or renters' policies and flag better options.
- **Decide: switch, stay, or renegotiate:** Use AI insights to act confidently.
- **Optimize credit usage:** Use alerts to pay down balances before statement close, boosting your credit score.

☑ *By month 6, you'll have streamlined insurance and strengthened credit, unlocking lower costs long-term.*

Months 7–8: Expand to Everyday Spending

- **Turn on smart shopper mode:** Enable automatic coupons, cashback, and reward optimization.
- **Set up price alerts:** For groceries, recurring household items, or major purchases.
- **Track shrinkflation:** Let AI flag package-size reductions and overpriced products.

☑ *By month 8, your AI is saving you money every time you shop— without lifting a finger.*

Months 9–10: Automate Long-Term Goals

- **Set a vacation or big-purchase goal:** Have AI break it into micro-savings.
- **Accelerate debt payoff:** Direct surplus savings toward your highest-interest balance.
- **Start investing automatically:** Use AI-driven micro-investing or auto-transfers into ETFs or index funds.

☑ *By month 10, your autopilot is no longer just saving—it's building wealth.*

Months 11–12: Future-Proof & Review

- **Add energy bill optimization:** Connect smart home tools or utility bill analysis.
- **Enable travel refund AI:** Automate price-drop monitoring and delay/cancellation claims.
- **Run your first annual review:** Have AI generate a year-end report of savings, wins, and next steps.

☑ *By month 12, you'll have a full-scale money autopilot: protecting, saving, and growing your finances 24/7.*

The Big Picture

This roadmap isn't about perfection—it's about progress. Each step builds on the last, layering automation so you're never overwhelmed. By the end of the year, you'll have:

- Stopped leaks you didn't even know existed.
- Turned small wins into hundreds—or thousands—of dollars saved.
- Laid the groundwork for long-term wealth building.

Takeaway: In just 12 months, you can go from financial guesswork to financial autopilot. By layering AI tools gradually, you create a system that protects, saves, and grows your money automatically—freeing you to focus less on numbers and more on living.

CONCLUSION

From Stress to Control

Recap of Key Savings Wins

Over the past chapters, you've seen how money quietly leaks out of everyday life—and how AI can step in to stop it. What used to take spreadsheets, discipline, and hours of research is now handled automatically. The result is not just a little extra cash here and there—it's a system that protects you, saves for you, and grows your wealth without constant effort.

Let's recap the biggest savings wins you've unlocked in this book:

Subscriptions: Stop Paying for What You Don't Use

- AI detects duplicate or unused subscriptions.
- Cancellations happen in one click or even automatically.
- Free trials are canceled before they ever hit your card.

Typical Savings: $200–$400 per year.

Bills: Beat Price Creep Before It Beats You

- Service providers raise rates quietly—but AI alerts you instantly.
- Negotiation scripts and chatbots roll back hikes in minutes.
- Case studies showed savings of hundreds from one renegotiation.

Typical Savings: $300–$600 per year.

Banking & Credit: Eliminate Hidden Fees

- AI flags overdraft fees, late fees, and unfair charges.
- Auto-generated dispute letters get charges reversed.
- Smart reminders prevent late payments, protecting credit scores.

Typical Savings: $100–$300 per year.

Insurance: Pay for Coverage, Not Loyalty Penalties

- AI compares policies across providers instantly.
- You know when to switch—and when staying is smarter.
- Annual optimization routine locks in fair prices.

Typical Savings: $200–$500 per year.

Everyday Shopping: Outsmart Retail Algorithms

- AI exposes shrinkflation, hidden markups, and dynamic pricing.
- Automatic coupons, cashback, and reward optimization layer savings on every purchase.
- Smart alerts notify you when prices drop.

Typical Savings: $300–$600 per year.

Fraud Protection: Stay One Step Ahead

- AI monitors accounts 24/7, catching scams and fake subscriptions.

- Alerts stop fraud in real time before money leaves your account.
- Family safety plans protect the most vulnerable members.

Typical Savings (losses prevented): $500–$1,000+ per year.

Budgeting & Forecasting: From Restriction to Guidance

- AI builds realistic, flexible budgets from your actual data.
- Forecasting predicts cash flow and bills before they hit.
- Automated savings goals make progress automatic.

Typical Savings: $100–$300 per year.

The Total Impact

When you add it all up, the average household can realistically expect to save **$1,000–$2,500 per year** by putting AI on autopilot. Some families will save far more, especially if they're carrying multiple subscriptions, rising utility bills, or overpriced insurance.

Takeaway: These savings aren't just one-time wins. They stack, compound, and grow into long-term wealth. By tackling subscriptions, bills, fees, insurance, shopping, fraud, and budgeting, you've created a system that reclaims money at every turn. And the best part? It runs in the background, freeing you from the stress of micromanaging every dollar.

The Mindset Shift: You Don't Manage Money, AI Does

For decades, the standard advice has been: *"Take control of your money. Track every expense. Stick to your budget."* And while that sounds empowering, the reality is exhausting. Life is too unpredictable, too busy, and too complex for most people to manually manage every financial detail. That's why so many give up on budgeting altogether.

The breakthrough of AI is that it flips this old equation: instead of you managing money, AI manages money for you.

From Stress to System

- **Old Way:** You set reminders to pay bills, then forget, then pay late fees.
- **New Way:** AI tracks due dates, pays automatically, and alerts you if something changes.
- **Old Way:** You scan bank statements for hidden fees.
- **New Way:** AI flags unfair charges instantly and even drafts dispute letters for you.
- **Old Way:** You juggle dozens of subscriptions, promos, and loyalty cards.
- **New Way:** AI cancels unused services, applies coupons automatically, and picks the best rewards card without you thinking about it.

The difference is not just in results—it's in peace of mind.

Why Letting Go Feels Hard

For some, the idea of "not managing money" feels risky. We're taught that financial responsibility means control, and control means constant attention. But true control doesn't come from micromanagement—it comes from building systems that work reliably whether you're paying attention or not.

Think about autopilot in an airplane. The pilot doesn't stop being in charge. They still set direction, monitor systems, and make adjustments when needed. But the routine, repetitive tasks are delegated to automation—because machines do them better. Your finances work the same way.

Trusting the System You Build

AI is not about blind trust. It's about building a transparent, rules-based system that you can oversee at a glance. Your role shifts from "accountant" to "supervisor":

- You set the goals.
- You approve the rules.
- You check in briefly to confirm everything is on track.

This shift frees up your mental energy for the things that matter—your work, your family, your future—while the AI handles the drudgery.

The Freedom in Letting Go

Ironically, the less you try to *control* every financial detail, the more in control you actually become. When AI catches fraud instantly, renegotiates bills before they spike, and quietly builds your savings in the background, you no longer live in constant financial stress. Instead, you gain something far more valuable than a balanced budget: confidence.

Takeaway: The future of personal finance isn't about tracking every penny—it's about designing systems that make good decisions for you, automatically. You don't manage money anymore—your AI does. And that shift doesn't mean losing control. It means finally experiencing it.

Motivation: What $1,000+ Saved Yearly Could Mean for Your Life

On paper, saving $1,000 a year might not sound life-changing. It's just $83 a month, or less than $3 a day. But in practice, that kind of money makes a massive difference—not just financially, but emotionally. Because it's not just about the dollars—it's about what those dollars *unlock*.

Immediate Relief

- **Fewer emergencies:** That $1,000 can cover a car repair, a medical bill, or a surprise expense without sending you into debt.
- **Less stress:** Knowing you have a financial buffer reduces the constant anxiety of living paycheck to paycheck.
- **More breathing room:** Even a small cushion means you stop juggling bills and start living with a sense of stability.

Lifestyle Upgrades

- **Travel:** $1,000 could cover a plane ticket for a vacation you thought you couldn't afford.
- **Education:** It could fund an online course, certification, or skill upgrade that boosts your earning potential.
- **Experiences:** It could mean more dinners out with friends, concerts, or family activities—memories instead of missed opportunities.

Long-Term Wealth

Here's where the real magic happens:

- If you simply save $1,000 per year, you'll have **$10,000 in a decade.**
- If you invest it with a modest 7% return, that becomes **nearly $14,000.**
- Over 30 years, it grows to **over $100,000.**

One small change—capturing the leaks AI finds for you—can snowball into a six-figure difference in your financial future.

The Emotional Payoff

Money saved isn't just numbers in an account—it's freedom. Freedom to say yes to opportunities. Freedom to leave a job you hate sooner. Freedom to handle life's curveballs without panic. Freedom to focus on goals, not survival.

AI doesn't just give you $1,000 back each year. It gives you back the *choice* of how to use it.

Takeaway: $1,000 saved yearly isn't small—it's transformational. In the short term, it creates breathing room. In the long term, it builds wealth. And with AI doing the heavy lifting, you don't just dream about what's possible—you actually make it happen.

QR Code: Bonus Resources, Printable Checklists, AI Tools

By now, you've built the foundation of your personal money autopilot. But your journey doesn't stop here. To make sure you can apply everything from this book quickly and easily, we've put together a set of bonus resources—all accessible through one QR code.

What You'll Get When You Scan

1. **Printable Checklists**
   - *Subscription Audit Checklist* – Review every recurring charge with one page of yes/no boxes.
   - *Insurance Optimization Checklist* – A step-by-step guide for your annual review.
   - *Fraud Safety Family Plan* – A quick-reference guide to share with parents, kids, or anyone you protect financially.
2. **AI Tool Recommendations**
   - A curated list of AI apps and services for subscriptions, bills, shopping, fraud alerts, and budgeting.
   - Direct links to trusted providers that use bank-grade security.
   - Free and low-cost options so you can start without financial risk.

3. **Mini-Guides & Templates**
    - o Negotiation scripts for bills and service providers.
    - o Email and phone templates for disputing fees.
    - o A 30-day AI-assisted budgeting worksheet to get results fast.
4. **Updates**
    - o As AI evolves, so will the tools. Scanning the code gives you access to updated recommendations and resources so your system never falls behind.

Why This Matters

This book gave you the knowledge. The resources give you the execution. Instead of rereading chapters to find key steps, you'll have everything in one place—ready to print, share, and use today.

Your Final Step

At the end of this chapter, scan the QR code. Save the link. Print what matters most. Share it with your family. And know this: you're no longer managing money alone. You've built an autopilot system—one that's supported by smart tools, practical checklists, and ongoing updates to keep your finances future-proof.

Takeaway: Knowledge creates awareness, but tools create results. With one QR code, you'll have instant access to checklists, AI apps, templates, and updates that keep your money autopilot running long after you close this book.

BONUS RESOURCES

List of Recommended AI Tools (with Disclaimers)

Below is a curated list of AI-powered tools and services that readers have found helpful for automating savings, spotting waste, handling bills, protecting against fraud, and generally letting your money operate on autopilot. Each entry includes what makes it useful *and* what to watch out for—so you pick tools that match your needs and stay safe and smart doing it.

Tool	What It Does Well	What to Check / Disclaimers
AI Subscription & Recurring Payment Scanners *(e.g. Subby AI, Trim, Truebill)*	Automatically scan your bank/credit card statements to find recurring charges, flag free trials, help cancel unsubscribed services. Great for recovering the "invisible subscriptions" you'd forget.	Check whether "read-only" connection is used (so the tool can't move money without permission). Be aware that "cancel on your behalf" features may require sharing more access or interacting with the service's support themselves. Sometimes services charge a fee or take a cut of savings—make sure you understand pricing.
Bill Negotiation / Rate Lock Tools *(e.g. Billshark, Rocket Money, some telco-specific tools)*	Tools that automatically find better offers, negotiate bills (internet, phone), or alert you when promotional rates are about to expire.	Availability depends on your provider / region. Negotiation attempts might affect service bundling, and sometimes the offers they lock in are temporary promos, not permanent rate reductions. Always verify new rate terms.

Tool	What It Does Well	What to Check / Disclaimers
Automated Budgeting & Forecasting Apps *(e.g. Cleo, YNAB with AI features, Monarch, FuturePay)*	Use your actual spending & income to build forecasts, set realistic budgets, predict cash flow, and allocate savings goals. Less manual entry, more adaptive guidance.	AI forecasts are only as good as the data given. If you have unusual months (large expenses, irregular income), the predictions may overshoot or undershoot. Always leave yourself buffer zones. Also understand how the tool syncs with your financial institutions—sometimes delays or categorization errors happen.
Shopping / Coupon / Cash-Back Extensions *(e.g. Honey, Rakuten, Capital One Shopping, PriceBlink)*	Automatically apply coupon codes, compare prices across stores, alert you to price drops, and apply cashback/rewards options. Great for everyday savings.	Many coupon tools require browser extensions or permissions—ensure they are from trusted sources. Some may track your browsing data; read privacy policies. Also, some "discounts" are inflated; they may drive you toward affiliates rather than objectively best deals.
Fraud Detection & Alerts *(e.g. Identity Guard, Experian alerts, some bank-integrated tools,*	Alerts when charges occur outside your regular patterns, when subscriptions appear you didn't authorize, or when suspicious activity is detected.	These tools can't prevent all fraud, especially highly sophisticated scams. They may generate false positives—some alerts you'll review and dismiss, which can feel

Tool	What It Does Well	What to Check / Disclaimers
dedicated AI fraud assistants)	Helpful 24/7 peace of mind.	noisy. Also, cost vs benefit: paid plans often provide more comprehensive coverage. Read the fine print about what "protection" actually includes (e.g. whether it helps with refunds, recovery, or just notifications).

How to Choose & Use These Tools

1. **Start with privacy & security.**
   Make sure the tool:
   - Uses encryption (e.g. SSL/TLS, 256-bit)
   - Offers read-only bank access if possible
   - Has strong authentication (2FA, etc.)
2. **Test one category at a time.**
   For example, try a subscription scanner first. Once you've canceled a few unused services and feel comfortable, layer in a bill negotiation tool or price comparison browser extension.
3. **Watch for fees.**
   Some tools are free; others take a commission on savings; others charge subscription fees. Ensure the annual value you expect is significantly greater than what you'll pay.
4. **Keep backups.**
   If a tool changes its business model (raises fees, changes access, or shuts down), have alternatives or manual copies of key info (like subscription lists, current bills).
5. **Stay in control.**
   Even automated features should allow you review & override actions. You don't want auto-cancellations or negotiations doing something you didn't intend.

Takeaway: Using AI tools is one of the clearest paths to reeling in savings, simplifying your financial life, and taking control. But they come with trade-offs. When you choose tools carefully, understand how they work, protect your data, and keep oversight, the benefits far outweigh the risks.

Ready-to-Use Negotiation Scripts

One of the easiest ways to save money is to **ask for it.** The problem is most people don't know what to say—or they freeze up when a customer service rep pushes back. That's why negotiation works best when you go in prepared with clear, polite, and confident language. Below are ready-to-use scripts you can adapt for your own bills, subscriptions, and services.

Script 1: Lowering Your Internet/Phone Bill

You:
"Hi, I noticed my bill went up by $X this month. I've been a loyal customer since [year], but I've seen better rates from other providers. Can you match or beat those offers so I don't have to switch?"

If they resist:
"I understand. But before I make a decision about switching, can you transfer me to the retention department to see if they can apply a loyalty discount?"

☑ Works best when: You've received a bill increase or know a competitor is offering a cheaper rate.

Script 2: Canceling a Subscription You Don't Use

You:
"Hello, I'd like to cancel my subscription effective immediately. I'm not using the service and I don't want to be billed moving forward."

If they push back with offers:
"I appreciate that, but I'm not interested in discounts or extensions. Please just confirm my cancellation today."

✅ Works best when: Services try to stall by offering free months or upgrades you don't want.

Script 3: Waiving a Bank Fee

You:
"Hi, I see a [$35 overdraft/late fee] on my account dated [date]. This doesn't reflect my usual banking activity, and I'd like to request a courtesy waiver."

If they refuse:
"I've been a customer for [X years], and I'd hate for this one charge to affect our relationship. Is there a supervisor I could speak with about reversing it?"

✅ Works best when: You rarely incur fees and can point to your loyalty.

Script 4: Insurance Renewal Negotiation

You:
"My policy is up for renewal, but I've found quotes from other providers that are significantly cheaper for the same coverage. Before I switch, can you review my account and see if you can match or beat those rates?"

If they resist:
"I understand. But I value consistency, and if you can adjust the premium, I'd prefer to stay with my current provider."

✅ Works best when: You run an AI-assisted policy comparison before renewal.

Script 5: Requesting a Refund for a Faulty Product or Service

You:
"I purchased [product/service] on [date], but it hasn't worked as advertised. I'd like a full refund, please."

If they resist:
"I understand company policy, but under consumer protection rules, I'm entitled to a refund when a product or service fails to perform as promised. Could you process that today?"

✅ Works best when: A company delivers something broken, delayed, or misleading.

Why These Scripts Work

- **Polite but firm:** You're respectful, but you don't back down.
- **Focused:** You state your request clearly—no long explanations or justifications.
- **Escalation-ready:** You always leave room to ask for a supervisor if needed.

And remember: AI can now generate these scripts for you automatically, tailoring them to your provider, situation, and even chat format. That means no more guessing what to say—just copy, paste, and save.

Takeaway: Negotiation doesn't have to be awkward. With the right script, you can save hundreds of dollars in minutes. Use these templates word-for-word or tweak them to fit your situation. The key is to ask with confidence—because the savings are there for the taking.

Bill Tracking Template (Spreadsheet or Notion Link)

One of the simplest but most powerful money-saving tools is a **bill tracker.** When you can see, in one place, every recurring bill—what it costs, when it's due, and when it last changed—you immediately eliminate surprises. A bill tracker also makes it easier to spot price creep and duplicate charges, so you're not caught off guard.

To make this effortless, we've included two versions of a ready-to-use bill tracking template:

- **Google Sheets / Excel version** – simple, flexible, easy to share.
- **Notion version** – interactive, searchable, and perfect if you already use Notion for personal organization.

What the Template Includes

1. **Bill Name & Provider** – e.g., Comcast Internet, Netflix, State Farm Insurance.
2. **Category** – Internet, Phone, Streaming, Utilities, Insurance, Banking, Other.
3. **Due Date** – Helps you avoid late fees by seeing what's coming up.
4. **Amount** – The current charge.
5. **Last Increase Date** – So you know when the price last went up.

6. **Notes/Actions** – For reminders like "Call to renegotiate" or "Trial ends this month."
7. **Status** – Active, Canceled, Negotiated, or Paused.

How to Use It

- **Step 1: Enter your current bills.** Add every subscription, utility, and recurring payment you can think of.
- **Step 2: Sort by category or due date.** This shows you where your money is flowing and when.
- **Step 3: Update monthly.** Enter any changes in amount or status.
- **Step 4: Use AI alongside it.** If you're using an AI finance tool, compare its subscription scan against your tracker. This double-check ensures nothing slips through.

Sample Columns (Spreadsheet View)

Bill/Provider	Category	Amount	Due Date	Last Increase	Status	Notes
Comcast	Internet	$89.99	12th	04/2023	Active	Eligible for renegotiation
Netflix	Streaming	$15.49	2nd	10/2022	Active	Consider cancel
Spotify	Streaming	$9.99	15th	01/2021	Canceled	Switched to family plan

---

Why It Works

Bills often feel chaotic because they're scattered—some in email, some in apps, some only on paper. A tracker consolidates them, giving you control at a glance. Combined with AI alerts, it becomes a powerful system: the AI catches changes, while your tracker ensures you never lose sight of the big picture.

Takeaway: A bill tracker is the simplest form of money autopilot—and when paired with AI monitoring, it becomes bulletproof. Use it once, and you'll never again be surprised by a bill creeping higher in the background.

Glossary

AI (Artificial Intelligence)

Computer systems designed to perform tasks that normally require human intelligence, such as analyzing patterns, predicting outcomes, or automating decisions. In this book, AI tools help you save money by spotting leaks, negotiating bills, and protecting against fraud.

AI Forecasting

The use of AI to predict future cash flow, expenses, and savings based on your past financial behavior. Unlike spreadsheets, forecasting adapts dynamically to changes in your spending.

AI Shopping Assistant

A browser extension or app that automatically finds coupons, activates cashback, compares prices, and recommends the best rewards card during checkout.

Autopilot Dashboard

A single screen where all your financial accounts, bills, subscriptions, and goals are tracked in real time—like a control panel for your money autopilot.

Automation (Financial)

The process of letting AI handle repetitive financial tasks for you, such as canceling subscriptions, transferring money into savings, or disputing fees, without requiring manual input every time.

Bill Creep

The gradual increase in monthly bills (like internet or phone) through small, often unnoticed price hikes.

Bundling (Insurance/Services)

Combining multiple policies or services (e.g., home + auto insurance, or internet + cable) to get a discounted rate. AI can analyze whether the bundle truly saves money.

Cashback

A program where you earn back a percentage of your purchases in cash or rewards. AI tools ensure cashback is applied automatically so you never miss savings.

Chargeback

A dispute process where a credit card company reverses a fraudulent or incorrect charge after you report it.

Credit Utilization

The percentage of your available credit that you're currently using. Lower utilization typically improves your credit score. AI alerts can help you pay down balances before your statement closes.

Deepfake

An AI-generated audio, image, or video designed to impersonate someone. Increasingly used in scams, such as fake "grandchild in trouble" calls.

Dynamic Pricing

An algorithm-driven system where online retailers adjust prices in real time based on demand, browsing history, or even your device type. AI shopping assistants expose these manipulations and secure fairer prices.

Emergency Fund

A dedicated savings account meant to cover 3–6 months of essential expenses in case of job loss, illness, or other emergencies. AI can build this fund gradually through micro-savings.

Encryption (256-bit)

A standard for data security that scrambles information so it cannot be read by unauthorized parties. Most financial AI tools use this level of encryption.

Fraud Detector (AI)

A system that monitors your transactions 24/7, spotting suspicious activity, unusual charges, or fake subscriptions in real time.

Loyalty Penalty (Insurance)

The hidden cost of staying with the same insurance provider for too long—companies often raise premiums on existing customers while offering discounts to new ones.

Micro-Savings

Small, automated transfers into savings accounts, often triggered by rounding up purchases or moving surplus funds on low-spend days.

Negotiation Script

Prewritten language (often AI-generated) that helps you confidently ask providers for lower bills, waived fees, or better rates.

Overdraft Fee

A bank charge applied when you spend more than your available balance. AI can flag overdraft risks early to prevent them.

Phishing

A fraudulent attempt (often via email or text) to trick you into giving away personal or financial information. AI email scanners catch these attempts more effectively than standard spam filters.

Price Creep (Retail)

A slow increase in the price of everyday goods, often disguised through shrinkflation or delivery markups. AI tools compare prices across stores to expose these increases.

Retention Department

A customer service division trained to keep customers from canceling or leaving. Often empowered to offer discounts or credits if you threaten to switch providers.

Round-Up Savings

An automated savings method that rounds up each purchase to the nearest dollar and deposits the difference into savings.

Shrinkflation

When a product's size or quantity decreases while the price stays the same. AI shopping tools can spot these changes.

Sucker List

A list of past scam victims circulated among fraudsters, making those victims more likely to be targeted again.

Subscription Audit

An AI-powered scan of your bank account or email that lists every recurring charge, helping you identify unused or duplicate subscriptions.

Tokenized Access

A security feature where AI tools connect to your bank through a secure digital token rather than storing your actual password. This ensures read-only access unless you approve transfers.

Two-Factor Authentication (2FA)

A security method requiring two forms of verification (e.g., password + text code) before granting account access. Essential for protecting financial apps.

Usage-Based Insurance (UBI)

A car insurance model where premiums are based on how much and how safely you drive. AI can recommend UBI if your driving patterns make you a candidate for lower rates.

Thank You

Thank you for reading *Save Money Using AI: Money Autopilot.* I wrote this book with one goal: to give you tools that actually *work*—not just theory, not just "try harder" advice, but a system that saves you money automatically and brings you peace of mind.

If you've made it this far, you've already taken the most important step: choosing to take control of your financial future. I'm grateful you trusted me to guide you, and I hope this book has given you not only practical savings, but also the confidence to know that you *can* win this game.

A Small Favor That Makes a Big Difference

If this book helped you, the best way you can support it is by leaving a review on Amazon. Reviews are how new readers discover books—and they make all the difference for independent authors like me.

Your review doesn't need to be long. Just a few sentences about what you found most useful (a tip, a tool, or even the mindset shift) can help someone else decide to take the leap.

Why Your Voice Matters

Every review not only helps this book reach more readers—it helps spread a movement. The more people who learn how to use AI to cut bills, cancel waste, and grow savings, the more financial freedom we create together.

Final Thought: You've already started building your money autopilot. Now, take a minute to leave your mark by sharing your experience. Your words could be the reason someone else saves $1,000+ this year—and builds the same sense of control you now have.

Thank you again. Here's to your growth, your savings, and your freedom.

THE

END

www.ingramcontent.com/pod-product-compliance
Lightning Source LLC
Chambersburg PA
CBHW071653210326
41597CB00017B/2198